ALASTAIR SAWDAY'S

Special
places to stay

FRENCH HOLIDAY HOMES

Edited by Clare Hargreaves

Typesetting, Conversion & Repro:	Avonset, Bath
Design:	Caroline King & Springboard Design, Bristol
Mapping:	Springboard Design, Bristol
Maps:	Bartholomew Mapping Services, a division of HarperCollins Publishers, Glasgow
Printing:	Butler & Tanner, Frome
UK Distribution:	Portfolio, Greenford, Middlesex
US Distribution:	The Globe Pequot Press, Guilford, Connecticut

Published in January 2002

Alastair Sawday Publishing Co. Ltd
The Home Farm Stables, Barrow Gurney, Bristol BS48 3RW
Tel: +44 (0)1275 464891 Fax: +44 (0)1275 464887
E-mail: info@specialplacestostay.com Web: www.specialplacestostay.com

The Globe Pequot Press
P. O. Box 480, Guilford, Connecticut 06437, USA
Tel: +1 203 458 4500 Fax: +1 203 458 4601
E-mail: info@globe-pequot.com Web:www.globe-pequot.com

First edition.

ISBN 1-901970-25-6 in the UK

ISBN 0-7627-2340-8 in the US

Printed in England

The publishers have made every effort to ensure the accuracy of the information in this book at the time of going to press. However, they cannot accept any responsibility for any loss, injury or inconvenience resulting from the use of information contained therein.

ALASTAIR SAWDAY'S

Special

places to stay

La Maison Neuve, entry no. 146

FRENCH HOLIDAY HOMES

The
Globe
Pequot
Press

Guilford
Connecticut, USA

ASP

Alastair Sawday Publishing
Bristol, UK

Contents

Contents

Acknowledgements

This has been a magnum opus. It is our first book on 'self-catering' - or 'holiday homes' - and starting from scratch has been a challenge. Clare Hargreaves has met many before, however, in a varied career which has included working for national newspapers, producing TV documentaries, writing a book on the cocaine trade, and leading walking holidays in France and Greece. So perhaps she was less daunted than many might have been. She has brought together a miscellaneous and fascinating collection of houses, of every conceivable French kind, and all of us who visit them will be grateful to her. We are grateful too for the huge amount of care she has taken in researching and writing about all the special places in this guide.

Behind the scenes are always other people. In this case our ever-loyal Ann Cooke-Yarborough oiled the wheels of Clare's machine by offering invaluable advice. Jo Boissevain was an administrative power-house and Annie Shillito a calm, cohering spirit behind it all. Thank you, too, to all the others who helped so much, especially to Julia Richardson for her indomitable strength and ability to bring order to a complex project.

Alastair Sawday

Series Editor:................ Alastair Sawday

Editor:......................... Clare Hargreaves

Managing Editor:......... Annie Shillito

Production Manager:.... Julia Richardson

Administration:............. Jo Boissevain, Rachel Brook, Laura Kinch, Marie Hodges

Accounts:..................... Jenny Purdy

Web editor:.................. Russell Wilkinson

Inspections:.................. Douglas Arestegui, Richard & Linda Armspach, Lillian Bell, Colin & Alyson Browne, Ann Cooke-Yarborough, Jill Coyle, Meredith Dickinson, John Edwards, Robin Fleet, Nina Freund, Georgina Gabriel, Susan Gill, Anna Halama, Clare Hargreaves, Diana Harris, Sue Hutton, Jo Bell-Moore, Caroline Portway, Sophie Tinnams, Elizabeth Yates

Additional research:...... Nina Freund

Regional photographs:.. Michael Busselle

Introduction

Welcome to a book which launches the start of a new series on self-catering accommodation, or vacation homes to our American readers. In the B&B guides, for which ASP has become loved, you stay in someone's home; in this one, you will still be staying in someone's home but they may live abroad, across the courtyard or in the other half of your house. Like other Sawday guides, this book is about people, for it is the people who mould the amazing houses in which you'll stay, and whose characters, eccentricities and generosity will make your holiday special.

There's a huge variety to chose from, from tiny *pigeonniers* and medieval watch-towers for two, to sumptuous châteaux (one with a four-poster bath!), and water mills where running rivers will lull you to sleep. We have a gold-mine in the Gard, and, in the Lot-et-Garonne, a converted railway station which still has the old train timetables on the walls. There are stone farmhouses where you can walk out of the front door and into the mountains, village houses tucked under the ramparts, and chic city apartments from where you can stroll to some of France's finest restaurants. There are bathrooms with gold taps and rustic houses which have only recently got electricity. Whatever you are looking for, more likely than not it will be within these book covers.

We've also provided a mixture of large and small properties, so that families, couples or groups of friends can all find something to suit them. There are places with pools big enough for several families with children, and *bijou* hideaways where a couple could happily spend a honeymoon.

The one thing our houses have in common is that they are special. This doesn't necessarily involve luxury, though you can find luxury here if you want it. Unlike most agencies which market self-catering cottages, we are unimpressed by the number of microwaves or colour televisions a property has. In some cases we may value it more highly if it doesn't have these but does have beautiful walks or is outstandingly peaceful, or has painstakingly preserved original age-worn terracotta floor tiles instead of modern factory-made ones. And we know, as you do, that people are often what makes a holiday, so, where relevant, we take them into account too. We assess each house on a far wider range of - highly selective - criteria, believing that 'quality of life' is based on much more than gadgetry.

What sets us apart from others who market holiday homes is that we don't just take the owner's word that a place is lovely: we check it out for ourselves. One of our inspectors has visited every house in this book to

Introduction

make sure it really *is* special. That way we hope we'll save you from nasty surprises like saggy mattresses which keep you awake at night or nearby, undisclosed building sites with roaring lorries which wake you rudely in the morning. We write our own copy too, so what you'll read is not advertising blurb but a description which is hopefully entertaining and honest. So if there's a main road nearby, or other rented cottages on the property, we'll say so loud and clear.

Our aim in selecting these holiday homes has been to allow you to experience the real France if you want to. So although you can rent a home where the furniture may have been bought in Habitat and the neighbours are English, we also offer you the chance to go totally French and to stay in villages where you'll be the only foreigners. In a few cases, you will need to speak in French to book them, so if you don't see a 'speaks English' symbol in their entry, pull out your phrase book. Around half our properties are French-owned, the rest belong to foreigners.

Finding the right place for you

Do remember to interpret what you read. If you are staying on a working farm or a vineyard expect cockerels to crow and tractors to rev at dawn. If you choose a "rambling château with old fashioned bathrooms" don't be surprised if the plumbing is idiosyncratic and gurgles in the night. If you're looking for a romantic getaway for two, don't select a place where the owners also do B&B (indicated by one of our symbols) or where there's another holiday cottage next door (indicated in the text). If you want to be able to stroll to the baker's in the morning to pick up croissants, don't choose a house in the sticks where shops are more than five kilometres away (also marked by a symbol). Likewise, if we say a place has white carpets and priceless ornaments it may not be the best house to take your inexhaustibly curious two-year-old .

Check on anything that is really important to you before confirming your booking, such as whether the swimming pool will be ready to use at Easter, or whether the bicycles have been promised to other guests or friends.

Do discuss any problems with your hosts at the time as they are the ones who can do something about it immediately. They would be mortified to discover afterwards that you were, for example, cold in bed when extra blankets could easily have been provided.

Introduction

How to use this book

Finding the houses

The entry number, in colour at the bottom of the page, is the number to use when looking for places on the map pages (at the beginning of this book). The other number in colour tells you on which map to find it.

Our maps

The General Map of France is marked with the page numbers of the Detailed Maps. The Detailed Maps show roughly where the Holiday Homes are and should be used with a large scale road map.

The address

We give only an abbreviated address for the property. Owners will supply complete addresses when you enquire or book.

How many does it sleep?

You'll see this shown on each page entry. In some instances we give two figures, divided by a dash. The first figure is the number of adults the house sleeps comfortably; the second is the number of people who can actually fit in, but the extras may need to sleep on sofabeds or on mezzanine floors. If you squeeze in the second number of people, don't be surprised if it feels cosy. If you want to bring extra people, you must ask the owner first. Otherwise, you could raise hackles - and even be in breach of contract.

Some places offer special rates if you are fewer people than the number shown. Often this applies only out of season.

Bedrooms

In this book a 'double' means one double bed, a 'twin' means two single beds. A 'triple' may have any mix of beds, and we give details where space allows. Extra beds and cots for children, sometimes at extra cost, can often be provided, so do ask. We also give details of bathroom arrangements, indicating when bathrooms are attached to one particular bedroom, and whether they are bathrooms or shower rooms. We don't give details of basins or bidets but do tell you how many toilets - 'wcs' - there are.

Prices

Now the Franc is history, we've given prices in Euros and/or Sterling, according to the wishes of the owner. If, like most of the owners, you still think in Francs there is a Euro/Franc/$/£ conversion table at the back of the book.

Introduction

The first figure is the price for one week's rental in low season (normally October to May), the second is the price for a week in high season (July and August). In certain areas, like ski resorts, high season is February.

Prices are for 2002 and may go up in 2003 so please check with the owner or on their website if they have one. A few properties offer a reduction if you stay for more than a week but don't expect any deals during peak season. Some places require you to stay a fortnight during these months.

Winter lets

Some holiday homes can be rented all the year round, some close during the winter, while others close during the winter but open for Christmas and New Year. The winter months are often a good time to glimpse the real France; the weather in the South can be very warm, and rates are normally extremely reasonable, so do consider renting in winter. In some cases, but not all, we tell you if winter lets are available, so please check with owners.

Gîtes and all that

Several of the places in this book are *gîtes ruraux*. There is no exact translation, but roughly it means a place to rent which is usually part of a farm or somebody's house. This goes back to the origins of the gîte movement which was created by the French government to provide employment for farmers' wives after the Second World War. Women had got used to working and were no longer content merely to keep the house. Many gîtes are registered with Gîtes de France, a government-controlled body which sets standards. Members display a green and yellow Gîtes de France symbol. For translations of other French terms for houses, please refer to the end of the book.

Symbols

Symbols and their explanations are listed on the last page of the book. They are based on the information given to us by the owners. However, things do change: a bike hire outlet may have gone out of business or the farmer next door may have sold his goats and no longer sell cheese. So please use the symbols as a guide rather than gospel and double-check anything that is important to you. In particular look out for the B&B symbol as this indicates that there may be other guests on the premises.

Introduction

Practical Matters

When to go

Families with school-age children will generally take their main holiday in July and August, which is when the French *en masse* will be taking theirs. So, for these months particularly it is essential to book well in advance.

If you can holiday outside those busy months, do so: it'll be slightly cooler (July and August can be unbearably hot); it'll be cheaper - often ridiculously so; you're less likely to get snarled up in traffic jams, especially on arrival and departure days (avoid 15 August, the Assumption bank holiday, at all costs); and most important of all, you have a better chance of seeing France going about its everyday life. May and June are the best months for flowers, for temperatures suitable for walking, and for visiting the Mediterranean coast. If mushrooms are your thing, then September's your month. Temperatures in autumn can be ideal, and the winter months, when you often get clear fine days, are well worth considering too (see Winter Lets above). A word of warning, though: some restaurants in rural areas only open in July and August. Some markets are also restricted to these months, but they tend to be the touristy, less authentic, ones anyway. Many restaurants close in the winter.

How to book

Contact the person listed on the entry under 'Booking details'. (You'll know what language to speak according to whether there's an 'English spoken' symbol or not.) They will normally send you a Booking Form or *Contrat de Location* (Tenancy Contract) which must be filled in and returned with the deposit, and commits both sides. On receipt of this, the owner will send a written confirmation and invoice, which constitutes the formal acceptance of the booking. Contracts with English owners are normally governed by English law.

Remember not to telephone later than 9pm or 9.30pm at the latest and that Ireland and the UK are one hour behind the rest of Europe. Country folk can be upset by enquiries coming through when they are fast asleep.

Deposits

British owners usually ask for a 25% deposit to secure a booking, though some charge less. This is non-refundable. It makes sense to take out a travel insurance policy with a cancellation clause to enable you to recover a non-refundable deposit. Your policy should also cover you for personal belongings and public liability.

Introduction

Many owners charge a refundable security/damage deposit, payable either in advance or on arrival.

Payment

The balance of the rent, and usually the security deposit, are normally payable at least eight weeks before the start of the holiday. (If you book within eight weeks of the holiday, you'll be required to make full payment when you book.) A few owners take credit cards and have our credit card symbol. Otherwise you will need to send a Euro cheque, or a Sterling cheque if the owner lives in Britain.

What payment covers

In most cases this covers electricity, gas and water. In some cases, the electricity meter will be read at the start and end of your stay and you will have to pay separately.

Linen is only included in the rent where our symbol says so, otherwise you will be charged extra. (Traditionally French owners have always charged extra for these, although this is changing.) Even where linen is provided, towels often are not, so please check when booking.

In some cases, owners charge for the cost of cleaning and you will have to pay this whether or not you are willing to clean the place yourself. At other places you can either clean yourself, or pay someone else to do it. In some cases tenants only have to pay for cleaning if they leave the house in a mess; the cost is deducted from the security deposit.

Some owners offer a discount for a two-week booking.

Changeover days

Usually this is a Saturday, but this varies so do check. Normally you must arrive after 4pm, and depart by 10am. Don't arrive earlier as your house may not yet be ready and you will wrong-foot your frantically busy owners.

What to take

Electric kettles are a rarity in French-owned homes, so if you're an addict, bring your own (with adaptor plug).

Children

Our symbol shows where children under the age of six are welcome. If there's no symbol, it doesn't mean the owner doesn't like children but may mean there is an unfenced pool or river, a large boisterous dog or some steep stairs. If you are convinced that your impeccably behaved five-year-old can cope, the owner may allow you to bring them - but at your own risk.

Introduction

Pets

More people will now be travelling to France with their pets. Our Pets symbol tells you which houses generally welcome them but you must check whether this includes beasts the size and type of yours; whether the owner has one too (will they be compatible?); and whether you can bring it in the house or must keep it in an outhouse. Your hosts will expect animals to be well-behaved and assume that you will be responsible for them at all times.

Electricity

You need a plug adaptor for the 220-volt 50-cycle AC current. Americans also need a voltage transformer (heavy and expensive) although some appliances are now made with bi-voltage capabilities.

Plugs and sockets

The old-style wall sockets, often rated at 600 watts, take two round prongs. The new kinds of sockets take fatter prongs and have a protruding earth (ground) prong. Go well armed with adaptors to cope with all eventualities.

Telephoning/Faxing

All telephone numbers in France have ten digits, e.g. (0)5 15 25 35 45. You should know that:

- the initial zero is for use when telephoning from inside France only, i.e. dial 05 15 25 35 45 from any private or public telephone.

- when dialling from outside France use the international access code (00 if you live in UK), then the country code for France - 33 - followed by the last 9 digits of the number you want, e.g. 00 33 5 15 25 35 45.

- numbers beginning (0)6 are mobile phone numbers;

- to telephone from France

  - to Great Britain: 00 44 then the code and number without the initial zero,

  - to the USA, dial 00 1 then the code and number without the initial zero.

- to ring Directory Enquires in France dial 12.

Télécartes (phone cards) are widely available in France and there are plenty of telephone boxes, even in the countryside, where you can use them. Few boxes now accept coins, and many take credit cards. Many of our holiday homes have telephones from which you can ring using a card.

Introduction

Business days and hours

If you get up late and stroll to the shops at midday hoping to pick up some tasty morsels for lunch, you won't eat. France closes down between midday (or sometimes 12.30pm) until around 2pm or 2.30pm for the all-important business of lunching. Whole communities turn into ghost towns while the nation munches. Some post offices have a crafty habit of even closing early for lunch, so don't get caught out. Most shops and banks open from 8am or 9am on weekdays, and food shops normally stay open until around 7.30pm. Many food shops open on Sunday morning but close on Mondays.

Environment

We seek to reduce our impact on the environment where possible by:

- Planting trees to compensate for our carbon emissions (as calculated by Edinburgh University); we are officially a carbon-neutral publishing company.

- Re-using paper, recycling stationery, tins, bottles, etc.

- Encouraging staff use of bicycles (they're loaned free) and encouraging car-sharing.

- Celebrating the use of organic, home and locally-produced food.

- Publishing books that support, in however small a way, the rural economy and small-scale businesses.

Subscriptions

Owners pay to appear in this guide; their fee goes towards the high production and publication costs of an all-colour book and of inspecting every single property. We really do only include places and owners that we find special, and plenty have failed to make it, though they were willing to pay. It is not possible for anyone to buy their way in.

www.specialplacestostay.co.uk

Our web site has online entries for many of the places in this book and in our other books, with up-to-date information and with direct links to their own email addresses and web sites. With this book in one hand, your mouse and a pen in the other and a cup of tea balanced precariously on top of your computer monitor, you'll be perfectly equipped to plan and book your trip. You'll find more about the site at the back of this book.

Introduction

Disclaimer

We make no claims to pure objectivity in judging our *Special Places to Stay.*
They are here because we like them. Our opinions and tastes are ours alone
and this book is a statement of them; we hope you will share them. We
have done our utmost to get our facts right but apologise for any mistakes
that may have crept in. Sometimes, too, prices shift, usually upwards, and
new buildings get put up.

Finally - *À vos plumes!*

Do let us know how you got on in these houses, and get in touch if you
stumble across others which deserve to be in our guide - we value your
feedback (good or bad) and recommendations enormously. Poor reports
are followed up with the owners in question, although we don't mention
the writer's name. Really bad reports lead to incognito visits after which
we may exclude a house. Recommendations may be followed up with
inspection visits. If yours leads to a place being included in a future edition,
you'll receive a free guide.

There is a report form at the back of the book or you can e-mail
frenchholidayhomes@sawdays.co.uk

I hope you will enjoy staying in these wonderful holiday homes as much
as we have enjoyed ferreting them out and meeting their owners, many of
whom have become friends. *Bonnes vacances!*

Finally, a French proverb to accompany you on your journey: *Des goûts et
des couleurs il ne faut pas disputer.* (There's no accounting for taste.)

Clare Hargreaves

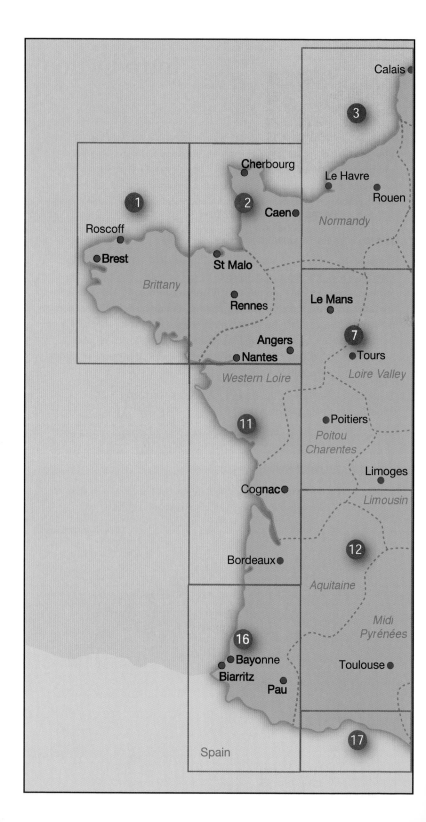

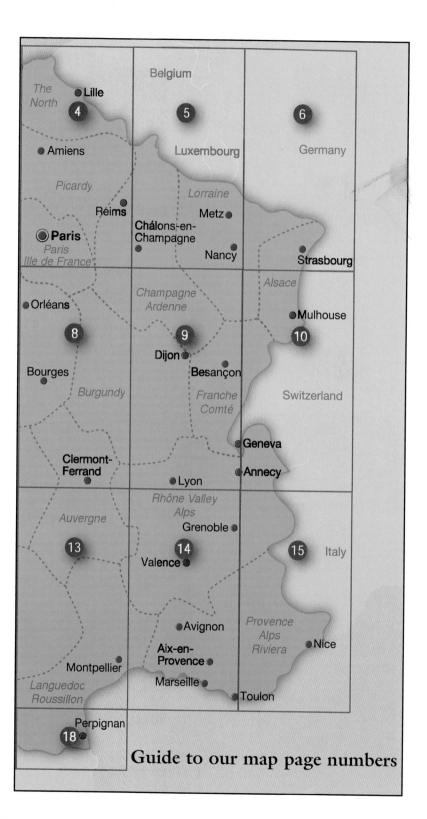

Guide to our map page numbers

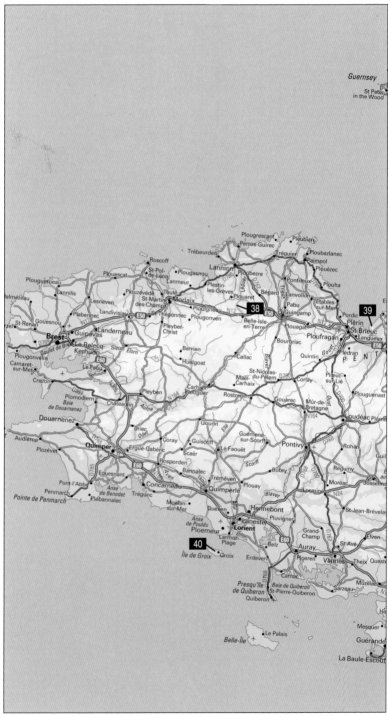

Scale for colour maps 1:1 600 000
(1cm:16km or 1 inch:25.25 miles)

Map 1

Map 2

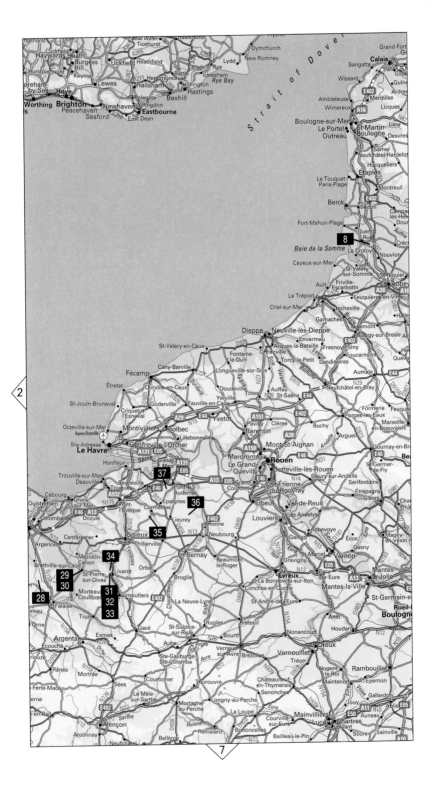

Map 3

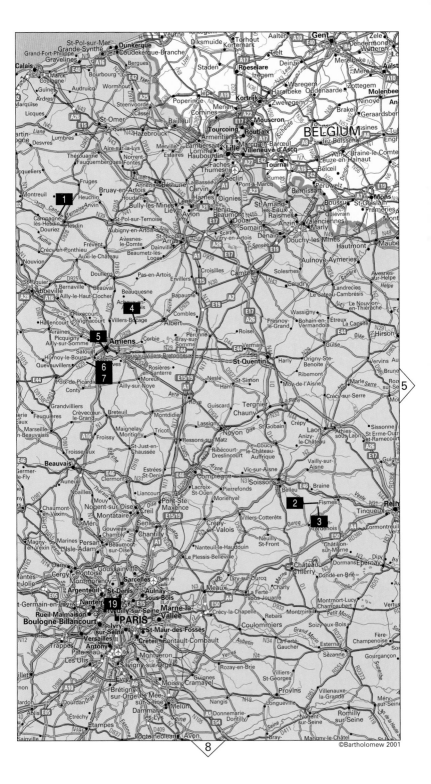

Map 4

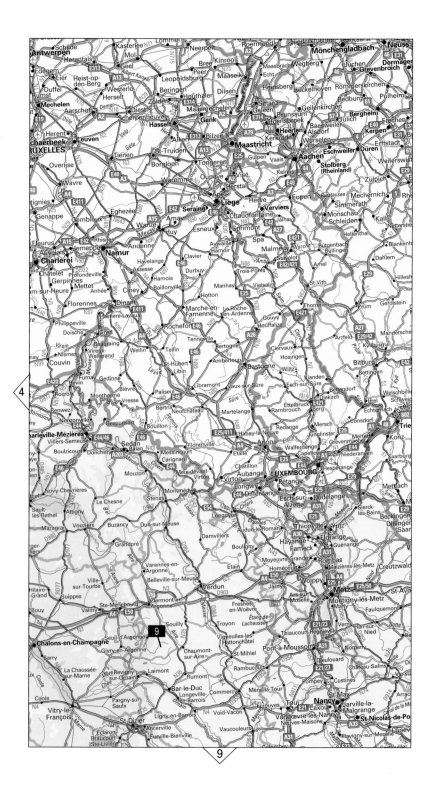

Map 5

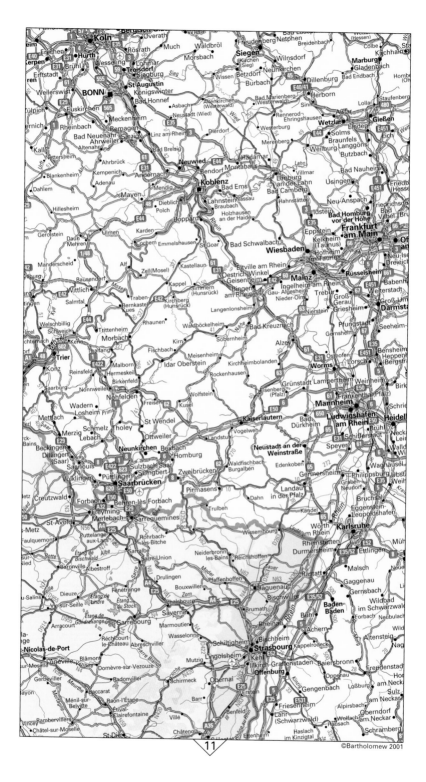

11

©Bartholomew 2001

Map 6

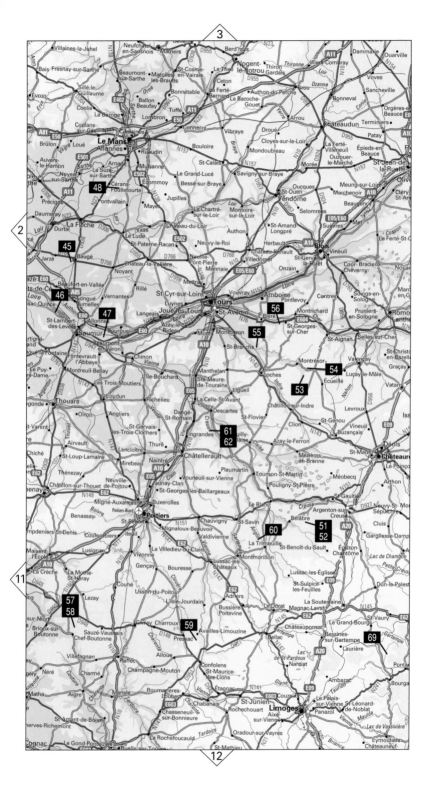

Map 7

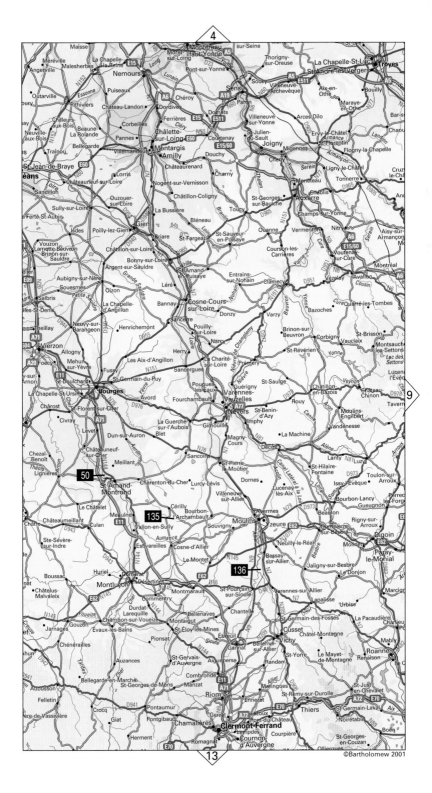

©Bartholomew 2001

Map 8

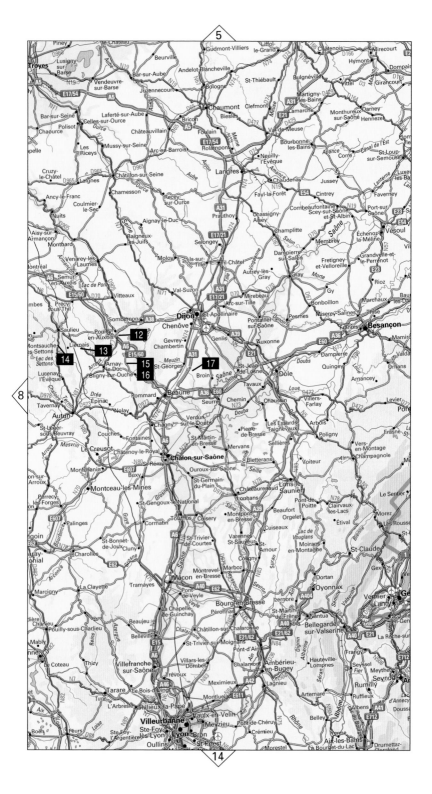

Map 9

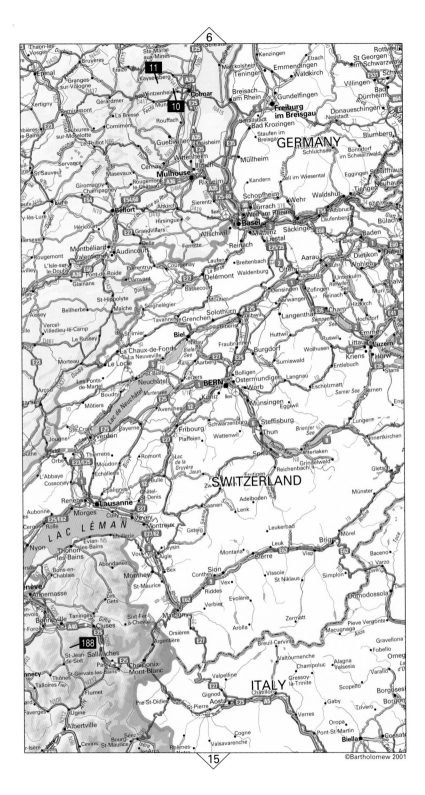

Map 10

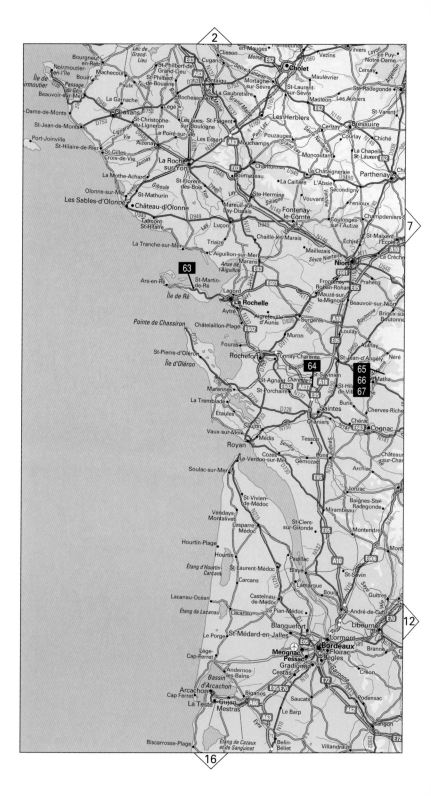

Map 11

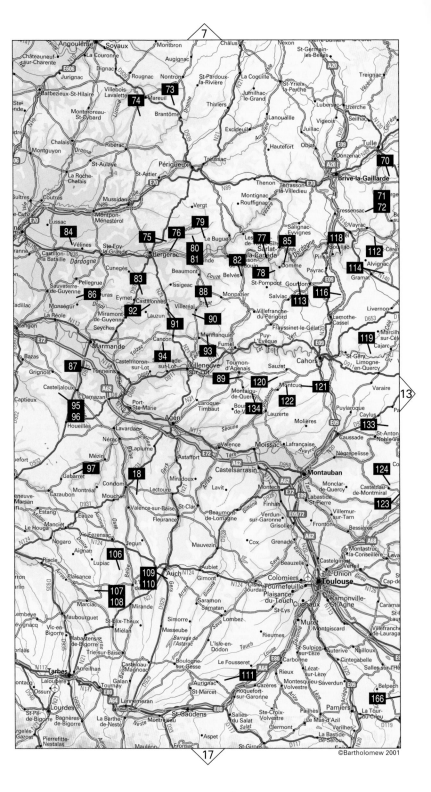

Map 12

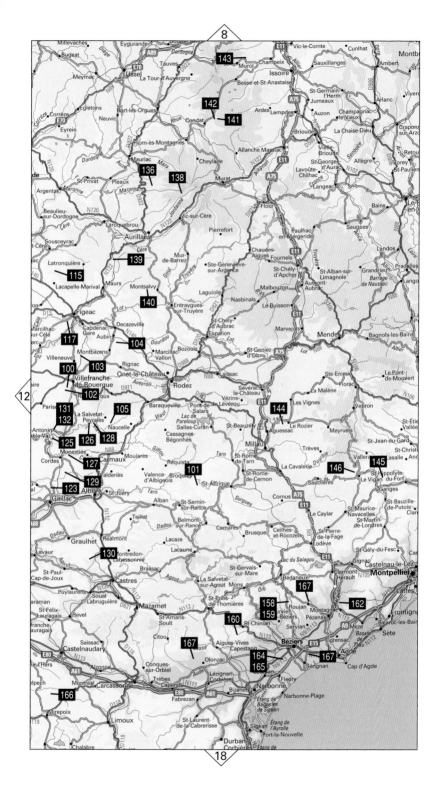

Map 13

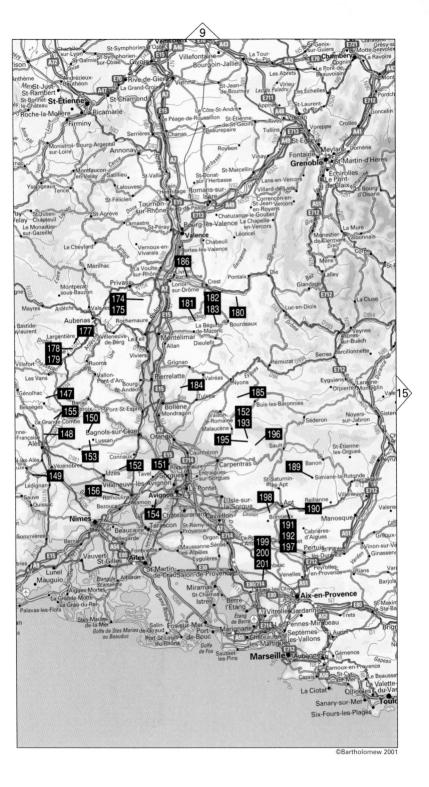

©Bartholomew 2001

Map 14

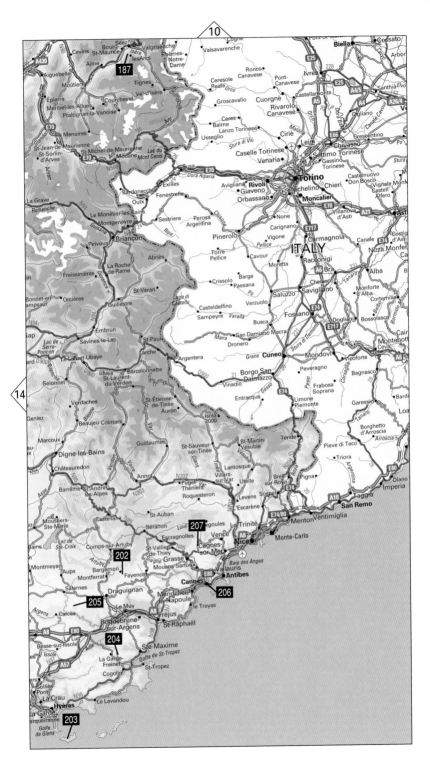

Map 15

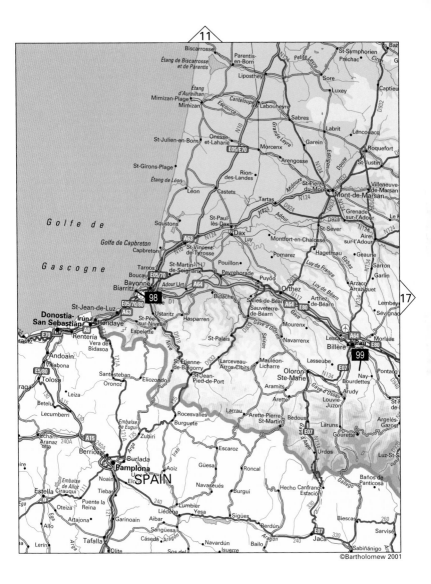

Map 16

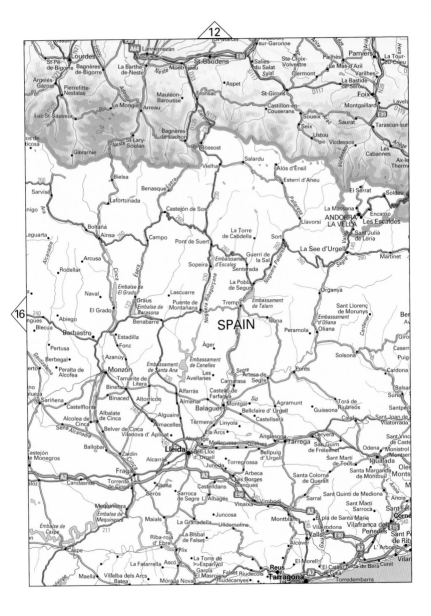

Map 17

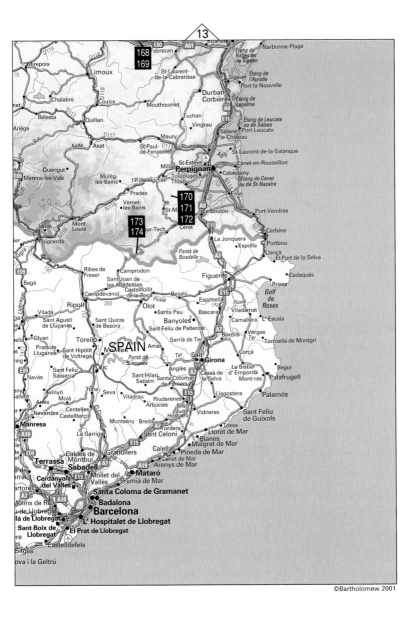

Map 18

The North
Picardy – Lorraine
Alsace – Burgundy
Paris – Ile de France

Photography by Michael Busselle.

La Hotoire, 62140 Guisy

Fabulously French, cosy and stylish, this studio apartment has been imaginatively converted from a 19th-century farm outbuilding by Martine and Marc-William. They abandoned high-powered jobs in Lille to seek peace in the country, and haven't looked back. Marc-William has blossomed as a painter (you can buy his work), and their enthusiasm for their rural life is infectious; they'll even lend you one of their friendly donkeys to accompany you on walks in the woods and fields surrounding the farm. Guests — up to 10 B&B guests may be here, too — are clearly a delight not a burden. The couple have proved their artistic talents in the decoration of this unpretentious little apartment: the ancient carved bed, daffodil yellow-velvet Voltaire chairs and a great antique *armoire* create a traditional rustic mood, and pretty floral print curtains and cushions pick out the blue of the walls. Dine in the courtyard, and roam in the long lush garden and paddock in the company of donkeys, hens and a tame cockerel.

Sleeps: 2-3.
Price: €240-€300.
Bedrooms: 1 double with extra single bed; shower & wc.

Booking details:
Martine & Marc-William Garrel
Tel: +33 (0)3 21 81 00 31
E-mail: a.la.hotoire@wanadoo.fr

Ferme de Ressons, 02220 Mont Saint Martin

Feel the simple country lives which have been played out within these old, old walls. There's nothing fancy or pretentious about this rustic farm cottage, with its ancient beams and neat brick fireplace. Come for its deep peace, soothing views and champagne vineyards and, if you wish, join Valérie and Jean-Paul and their B&B guests for delicious dinners cooked in the grand farmhouse across the gardens from home-grown produce (ask in advance). Or gather around the old square wooden table in your simple kitchen with its incongruously grand Henri II dresser. Other rooms have an eclectic mix of antique and modern furniture, including one of the bedrooms with its 'interesting' wallpaper in red, green and blue horizontal stripes, green quilted bed and butter-yellow curtains. Fish in the pond if you bring your own permit and rod; the hilly forests of the Montagne de Reims, south-east of here, provide unexpectedly rich walking and a sharp contrast to the flat vineyards. The beech woods at Verzy are believed to be over 500 years old.

Sleeps: 6.
Price: €230-€285.
Bedrooms: 1 double with basin;
2 twins; bathroom & wc.

Booking details:
Valérie & Jean-Paul Ferry
Tel: +33 (0)3 23 74 71 00
Fax: +33 (0)3 23 74 28 88

Map no: 4

Le Point du Jour, 02220 Mont Saint Martin

Valérie, the French owner, is an architect and has left her artistic stamp on the house's attractively simple rooms, with their lovely antiques and views over the champagne vineyards. This 19th-century village house, two kilometres from the Ferry's farm, exudes light, space and homeliness. The living room has beams, an old piano and a modern, round, glass and chrome dining table. Upstairs, there are parquet floors, pretty woven cotton curtains with floral patterns, and a splendid, ornately carved 19th-century Portuguese bed. One twin has more sober country-style beds, with sunflower-yellow covers and curtains, and sloping ceilings. Dine out on the south-facing terrace or in the garden, from where you can stride straight out into fields and woods. Or head for one of the many Champagne *maisons* in Reims, a 20-minute drive away, and taste the bubbly stuff. Those of Mumm, Taittinger and Piper-Heidseick allow you to join (paying) tours without an appointment, including a *dégustation*.

Sleeps: 6.
Price: €245-€380.
Bedrooms: 1 double with own bathroom; 2 twins; shower; wc.

Booking details:
Valérie & Jean-Paul Ferry
Tel: +33 (0)3 23 74 71 00
Fax: +33 (0)3 23 74 28 88

Les Aulnaies, 80260 Bavelincourt

The lovely red bricks of this 19th-century stable block are as warm as the welcome of your hosts. Madame, usually followed by a brood of grandchildren, bustles and nurtures, while Monsieur quietly smiles. Retired farmers, they live in the imposing manor house — red brick too — where they lodge B&B guests. Find your own private corner in the huge garden across the road, with its plane-tree avenue leading to a lily pond and grotto which children will love. Inside, the mood is of comfortable elegance. Dark, mostly antique, furniture, and golden curtains and furnishings stand out against the pure white walls and beige tiled floor in the living/dining room, and the kitchen is both pretty and practical. Bedrooms under the sloping roof rafters (once the hayloft), are fresh and cheerful with carefully considered colour schemes, floral touches, and deliciously thick carpets. Dine out in the communal courtyard. The World War One battlefields are nearby, and you can visit the fascinating Historial de la Grande Guerre museum in Péronne on the Somme.

Sleeps: 6 + 1 baby.
Price: €305-€380.
Bedrooms: 2 doubles, 1 with cot;
1 twin; bathroom & wc.

Booking details:
M & Mme Noel Valengin
Tel: +33 (0)3 22 40 51 51
Fax: +33 (0)3 22 71 22 68
E-mail: accueil@somme-tourisme.com

Map no: 4

Le Clos Alexandre, 80000 Amiens

The scent of lilac and lavender will waft you to sleep in this floral paradise, crafted in 1932 by Nicole's father, Alexandre. Started as a huge vegetable garden and orchard with 400 types of fruit trees, it has been totally redesigned by Nicole, who rescued the garden from two decades of neglect. It now has more than 1500 varieties of trees and shrubs, many of them rare. The gardens open to the public on summer afternoons, but at dusk you'll reclaim their magical tranquillity for yourself. The wood-and-brick house is a 50-year-old hunting lodge where Nicole's father brought his friends for liquid merriment after hunting expeditions, and you'll spot medieval hunting motifs on the living room terracotta floor tiles. Wooden-framed ceilings, antique or pine furniture and 19th-century paintings combine to create a quaint old-fashioned atmosphere. The long, thin, simply-furnished bedroom is reached by external stone steps and snuggles under the roof rafters. There's an excellent restaurant within walking distance. Gardeners will be in heaven.

Sleeps: 2-4.
Price: €380-€430.
Bedrooms: 1 double with 2 extra single beds; bathroom & wc downstairs.

Booking details:
Nicole Lemaître
Tel: +33 (0)3 22 95 19 71
Fax: +33 (0)3 22 38 91 50

26 rue Principale, 80480 Creuse

Monique used to run an antique shop and throughout this beautiful cottage rooms carry the mark of a woman of taste, discretion and quiet confidence. Ancestral portraits line the walls, fabrics are pretty and high quality, and carefully selected pieces of old furniture create a mood of sober, clutter-free elegance. In the living/dining room clean white walls reinforce the warm-coloured terracotta tiles and classic blue-and-white check gingham tablecloths and curtains. Bedrooms too are decorated in a smart country style with a perfect mix of antiques and contemporary furnishings, including blue and white stencilled bedheads. Softly-spoken Monique runs a B&B and, at certain times of year, painting workshops — why not join in? Enjoy the company of bantams and a bouncy black Labrador in the huge gardens, or visit Amiens and its fascinating network of canals and *hortillonnages* (market gardens). The Saturday morning riverside market overflows with produce of the area's fertile land.

Sleeps: 4.
Price: €380-€430.
Bedrooms: 1 double; 1 twin; bathroom & wc.

Booking details:
Monique Lemaître
Tel: +33 (0)3 22 38 91 50
Fax: +33 (0)3 22 38 91 50

Map no: 4

26 rue Principale, 80480 Creuse

The soft light filters through the trees of the lovely garden, luxuriant and serene. With its neat tended beds to the front, and rough, wild area behind, the garden will inspire anyone who stays in this little studio. Eat out on the terrace, snooze on the lawns, explore the secret woody corners. The studio, like a nest in the roof of the 200-year-old stable buildings, has been stylishly converted by French owner Monique who lives in the timbered manor house next door. It's snug, neat and simple, with a colour scheme of marine blue and white, and pure white walls offset by a solid antique table and attractive gilt-framed paintings. The other rented cottage is below, and B&B guests sleep in neighbouring rooms, but the atmosphere is discreet and you're unlikely to be disturbed. Come here to rest, to roam, and to enjoy the quiet company of Monique. If you want to go further, Amiens's 13th-century Gothic Cathedral — the largest in France — is a must and the sea is just a 35-minute drive. Lovers will love it.

Sleeps: 2.
Price: €150-€230.
Bedrooms: 1 double with shower & wc.

Booking details:
Monique Lemaître
Tel: +33 (0)3 22 38 91 50
Fax: +33 (0)3 22 38 91 50

Map no: 4

Le Thurel, 80120 Rue

A purist's paradise. Outside, it's aristocratic and ever-so-white; inside, a minimalist's dream, life stripped to the bare essentials. This farm cottage will delight those who enjoy clutter-free living, austerity and space. Scrubbed floorboards and clean white walls are enriched by the odd splash of colour from a rug or table-cover. The huge living/dining room is decorated in ivories, creams and beiges — in beautiful contrast with the smokey blue-grey window frames and the antique dining table and chairs. Enjoy views of the courtyard and a stunning red-brick barn in front; and behind, the large leafy garden which you share with the Bree-Leclef's B&B guests. Bedrooms are white (of course) with fabulously luxurious linen. Belgian Patrick and Claudine will go out of their way to initiate you into the local lore. No surprise to learn he is an interior architect; she is an ex-teacher of Italian and concocts divine suppers which you're welcome to share. *Cleaning charged on top.*

Sleeps: 6-7.
Price: €665.
Bedrooms: 2 doubles, 1 with extra single bed; 1 twin; bathroom; wc.

Booking details:
Claudine & Patrick Van Bree-Leclef
Tel: +33 (0)3 22 25 04 44
Fax: +33 (0)3 22 25 79 69
E-mail: lethurel.relais@libertysurf.fr
Web: www.lethurel.com

Map no: 3

La Cabane

Like Machu Picchu this extraordinary collection of dwellings lay undiscovered by modern man for a long time. Tucked out of sight on a hill plateau — in this case to avoid the eagle eyes of the planners – it led a quiet and probably illegal existence until our eagle-eyed inspector found it while looking for a stray goat. There is room inside for several families, in a cunningly contrived set of interconnecting rooms. The second floor was a recent addition, an impressive triumph of hope over other people's experience. Our inspector was struck by the conceptual similarity to the 'Pueblo' Indian dwellings in North America and some of the great communal buildings of India. All is hugger-mugger, economical, efficient, perfect for a tightly-knit community. Local materials were scavenged for the construction, which took place over a long period. Nothing is wasted. The bathroom is straightforward, spartan, cleverly open to the elements. A rare find.

Sleeps: 5-50, according to tolerance.
Price: No money required, but initiation necessary. A dunk in the mud followed by a cold *al fresco* bath is payment aplenty.
Bedrooms: One, open-plan in extreme.

Booking details:
The Elders
Tel: Contact by pigeon or stone tablet
Fax: Didn't understand the word
E-mail: sleep@anawkwardangle.fr
Web: www.dontbesosilly.fr

Vignoble Klur, 68230 Katzenthal

You'll live, drink and breathe wine here: the Klur family has been running these vineyards for generations, and a green sea of vines surrounds the pretty half-timbered Alsacian village in which this sedate yellow house stands. In this ex-wine merchant's home, the Klur family live downstairs letting the first-floor as an apartment. Indulge in a little *dégustation* of the family's varied wines (including their prized Grand Cru Wineck-Schlossberg) from the huge oak barrels in the *cave* next door. Large and light, the flat has beautiful rug-strewn polished wooden floors and a pleasing mix of modern and antique furniture. White walls with delicate stencilling contrast with William Morris green door frames and ceiling beams. Wake in the morning to the braying of the Klur's donkey, Kougelhopf, who will, if you wish, accompany you with a picnic into the Vosges mountains. There are footpaths straight from the door, but if you don't feel like walking, there's the garden to relax in — or there might just be a few more wines to try.

Sleeps: 2.
Price: €335.
Bedrooms: 1 double with shower & wc. Cot on request.

Booking details:
Francine & Clément Klur-Graff
Tel: +33 (0)3 89 80 94 29
Fax: +33 (0)3 89 27 30 17
E-mail: info@klur.net
Web: www.klur.net

Map no: 10

Les Hirondelles, 68370 Orbey

Nature lovers will not want to leave. Swallows and redstarts nest in the eaves, deer populate the forests, and all around are breathtaking views across the Rhine Valley to the Black Forest. In summer walk into the mountains from the front door, in winter don your skis and, in the periods in between, head for the *Route de Vin* to sample the area's excellent wines. Some of the fiercest fighting in both world wars took place here. You'll see World War Two bullet-holes in the farmhouse where English owner John runs a B&B, and front-line trenches from World War One and a museum are a 10-minute drive away. The little converted granite barn is comfortable and cosy with panelled walls, wooden floors and simple pine furniture. In summer the locals compete for the best scarecrow and you'll see them in all shapes and sizes. Be sure to visit the stunning medieval walled village of Riquewihr, and buy Munster cheese from the farm shop opposite.

Sleeps: 4-7.
Price: €458.
Bedrooms: 1 double plus extra single; 1 twin; 1 double sofabed; shower & wc.

Booking details:
John Kennedy
Tel: +33 (0)3 89 71 34 96
Fax: +33 (0)3 89 71 34 96
E-mail: JhKenl@aol.com

Map no: 10

Château de Créancey, 21320 Créancy

In the grounds of a breathtakingly beautiful château, with a moat running past the kitchen door and, opposite, its very own *pigeonnier* with a resident owl, this listed 14th-century tower is a truly special place. Fiona — ex-Sotheby's — and her French husband, Bruno, have restored it with impeccable taste and passionate respect for the building's original materials and character. Arrow slits — surprisingly light — are your windows, and an old wooden staircase twists its crooked way upstairs. French country furniture, quarry-tiled floors and muted pink walls create a mood of warm elegance in the spotless living/dining room, and in the double bedroom upstairs you'll still see the original 14th-century beams. There's a small oak fitted kitchen with flagstone floors and basic cooking facilities (no oven). Eat on the terrace by the moat to the sound of hoopoes, and enjoy some local Burgundy wines. Explore the rugged Côte d'Or and châteaux on foot or by bicycle. *Château does B&B. Children must be able to swim.*

Sleeps: 4.
Price: €460-€610.
Bedrooms: 1 double; 1 twin; shower & wc.

Booking details:
Fiona de Wulf
Tel: +33 (0)3 80 90 57 50
Fax: +33 (0)3 80 90 57 51
E-mail: chateau@creancey.com
Web: www.creancey.com

  Map no: 9

La Maison de Grandmère, 21430 Liernais

The stoneware plates and bowls are made by the American owners who run a pottery in nearby Vandenesse-en-Auxois; their artistic touch is evident in the beautiful yet simple furnishings of this lovely farmhouse. They follow a long tradition of craftsmanship, for the house once belonged to the clog-maker — you'll see his bench in the old workshop — and these villages in the Morvan National Park are well known for their crafts. Unwind after a day's walking or birdwatching around the farmhouse table in the homely terracotta-floored dining room/kitchen, with cheerful ceramic wall tiles and the original stone sink and bread oven. The Williams have skilfully and unselfconsciously kept the feel of a 1920s farmhouse, particularly in the bedrooms which still have the original rose-sprigged wallpaper, antique beds and handmade patchwork bedcovers. Foodies and wine buffs will be in heaven: Saulieu, with its famous Côte d'Or restaurant, is nearby, as are numerous Burgundy wine *caves*.

Sleeps: 6 + 1 baby.
Price: €340-€610.
Bedrooms: 1 double; childrens' room with 1 double & 2 singles; bathroom; wc.

Booking details:
Mary Williams
Tel: +33 (0)3 80 49 29 19
Fax: +33 (0)3 80 49 29 19

Map no: 9

Maison de la Salamandre, 21430 Savilly

Pretty Savilly straddles the rolling hills of the north-eastern edge of the Morvan National Park. Morvan is a Celtic word for black mountain and a giant slab of granite which gives the Park its name. Magnificent views over the Park are one of the many highlights of this beautiful 1800 farmhouse and barn, splendidly isolated but near the village. Luxuriously and stylishly restored by its Anglo-Dutch owners, another highlight is the Great Room, a vast oak-beamed converted barn, so called because that's what guests exclaim when first entering it. The stone fireplace, modelled on a Gaudi arch, was crafted by a master stone mason who worked on the famous architect's Sagrada Familia Cathedral in Barcelona. Cool, light and modern, come here to meditate, chat or to relax after a hot day by the pool. The house is similar in style, with pure white walls, clean lines and a happy mix of modern and antique furniture. You'll spot artefacts from Asia, where the owners lived before moving to a village 20 minutes away. Explore the National Park by foot along the GR13. A real treat.

Sleeps: 6-7.
Price: €950-€1,600.
Bedrooms: 2 doubles; 1 twin; 1 single daybed in 'Day Room'; shower room.

Booking details:
Hulya & Chris Gray
Tel: +33 (0)3 80 84 15 47
Fax: +33 (0)3 80 84 15 47
E-mail: discoverburgundy@hotmail.com
Web: www.discoverburgundy.com

Map no: 9

Rose Cottage, 21360 Painblanc

The best of Burgundy: vineyards, gastronomic eateries and the Morvan Regional Park are all within reach, and here in Painblanc (literally, white bread) you'll get a taste of tranquil village life where the biggest event of the week is the visit of the butcher's and baker's vans. Prettily draped in wisteria and roses, this 19th-century stone village house has been beautifully restored by English owners Penny and Ben who live in a nearby village. The centrepiece is the kitchen, sunny and homely, with a large wooden table to gather around for feasts in front of the woodburner. The original hexagonal terracotta floor tiles and handsome oak beams have been kept, as have the endearingly sloping floors of the apricot and cream bedrooms. The downstairs bathroom has foot imprints of humans and geese. Take lazy, long lunches under the enormous willow tree in the lovely large garden and orchard, with its pond full of vocal frogs. Shop in pretty Bligny sur Ouche which also has a narrow gauge steam railway.

Sleeps: 7 + 1 baby.
Price: €415-€540.
Bedrooms: 1 double; 1 twin; 1 triple plus cot; bathroom; shower; 2 wcs.

Booking details:
Penny & Ben Martin
Tel: +33 (0)3 80 20 19 13
Fax: +33 (0)3 80 20 19 13

Map no: 9

Well Cottage, 21360 Painblanc

"No herbicides here, just cowslips, lady's smock and wild orchids. Amazing," wrote one guest who stayed at this pretty 19th-century stone cottage in early summer. In autumn enjoy the turning colours in the woods and, if you're lucky, spot deer, red kite and buzzards. Whenever you come, you'll love the cottage's long lazy views over the garden to fields and the upper part of this tranquil village. Among a cluster of cottages and farm buildings on a quiet side street, it's been attractively restored by English owners Penny and Ben. Oak beams — old, vast and welcoming — dominate the large living/dining room/kitchen which has attractive features like a little stone alcove and a window seat. There's a modern terracotta tiled floor and the sitting area, in primrose yellow, has a comfy sofa, *chaise longue* and Godin woodburner. An open oak staircase leads to simple carpeted bedrooms, with sloping beamed ceilings and velux windows. Explore the area on foot or by bicycle, or do some wine-tasting in the famous Burgundy vineyards of the Côte de Nuits.

Sleeps: 4-5.
Price: €325-€445.
Bedrooms: 1 double with extra single;
1 twin; shower; wc.

Booking details:
Penny & Ben Martin
Tel: +33 (0)3 80 20 19 13
Fax: +33 (0)3 80 20 19 13

  Map no: 9

Les Hêtres Rouges, 21700 Argilly

The mood is traditional, the furniture antique, and the gardens stretch serenely as far as the eye can see: little would seem to have changed since the Duke of Burgundy came here at weekends to hunt. The past is something Madame Bugnet is well versed in: she used to run an antique shop, and restoring old buildings is her passion. When not busy caring for her B&B guests in the hunting lodge next door, she has put her artistic talents to good use in renovating and decorating this lovely wisteria-draped outbuilding. Downstairs rooms are a festival of warm ochres, pinks and blues which enhance the lovely antique furniture, and there's a fine working fireplace. The upstairs bedroom has a handsome brass bed, rich colourful fabrics and interesting artefacts. If you're a wine buff you'll know the names of the surrounding villages like Nuits Saint Georges and Pommard already; visit their *caves* for a tasting if your purse allows, or explore the pretty Côte d'Or along the GR7 and GR76 footpaths.

Sleeps: 2-3.
Price: €1,141 (3rd person €217 supp.).
Bedrooms: 1 double with extra single bed, bathroom & wc.

Booking details:
Jean-Francois & Christiane Bugnet
Tel: +33 (0)3 80 62 53 98
Fax: +33 (0)3 80 62 54 85
E-mail: leshetresrouges2@wanadoo.fr
Web: www.leshetresrouges.com

Hameau de Pourio, Roquepine 32100

Light, stone and natural fabrics characterise this unpretentious and utterly tranquil barn conversion. One of a cluster of farmhouses at the end of a track, it's been in the Latour family for generations. They live in Bordeaux so the neighbour (the hamlet's only permanent inhabitant) will let you in. The huge living and dining rooms are simply furnished with wooden, cane or rush-seated chairs, sisal floor mats and exposed pale stone walls. Roof beams are paintwashed in grey and there's a fireplace adorned with family trinkets. Throughout, dreamy white curtains hang from tree branch poles and are tied back with raffia. Unusual metal stairs lead to a mezzanine floor (with extra single bed) and the upper floor. Bedrooms are sparsely furnished like the rest of the house, with white walls and bedcovers. Eat out on the cobbled terrace or relax in the garden among the fruit trees. There's plenty to see in this beautiful area: Condom and Armagnac are nearby and there's excellent walking and cycling.

Sleeps: 7-8.
Price: €350-€550.
Bedrooms: 2 doubles, 1 with own bathroom & wc; 1 twin; 1 single & cot; bathroom; wc.

Booking details:
Denis Latour
Tel: +33 (0)5 56 24 39 82
Fax: +33 (0)5 56 91 71 55

10 rue du Jour, 75001 Paris

The Louvre, St. Eustache Church and Rue Montorgeuil, one of the best street markets in Paris, are all within a five-minute walk from this small, central 17th-century apartment. Stay for a fortnight and become a real Parisian: greet your French neighbours on the stairs as you nip out to buy the morning croissants, sample some of Paris's best-loved restaurants (including Le Pied du Cochon, a survivor from the Sixties when Les Halles was still a wholesale market), and top up your wardrobe from the *grands magasins*. You'll climb 95 steps to get to this fourth-floor flat but the roof terrace makes it all worthwhile. Enjoy panoramic views of Paris's granite rooftops and sip a well-earned aperitif among its terracotta pots. Long and thin, the flat is comfortably decorated with modern pine furniture and prints by 20th-century artists. The kitchen/dining room has a warm, pleasing terracotta tile floor, while the sitting room has a parquet floor and stately mirrors which enhance the sense of space. *Minimum two week stay.*

Sleeps: 2-plus.
Price: €686 per fortnight.
Bedrooms: 1 double; 1 sofabed in living room; 1 bathroom.

Booking details:
Clare Ash
Tel: +44 (0)207 607 4989
Fax: +44 (0)207 700 7446
E-mail: clarebyday@aol

Normandy

Photography by Michael Busselle.

La Bergerie, 50580 Saint Remy des Landes

After a day on the dunes, cook your dinner, Norman-style, in the great inglenook fireplace, and wash it down with a flask of local cider. All is wooden inside this ancient farmhouse, from the gorgeous panelling around the hearth to the inviting oak settle and heavy ceiling beams. The high-quality, personalised furnishings make this feel like a much-loved home rather than a holiday let — probably because it *is* a home much of the year. Even though the Lea family won't be here when you are, they'll make you feel welcome on arrival by leaving you food and drinks. Enjoy serene views over the house's eight acres of fields from the huge, south-facing master bedroom; children will be in heaven in the carpeted, primrose-coloured dorm. There's a games room if it's wet; if not, head for nearby Portbail to swim, sail or ride. If you're not persuaded to cook (despite the lovely Paul Bocuse range in the well-equipped kitchen), try the *moules* in the town's many restaurants. Ideal for two families holidaying together. Temptingly close to Britain.

Sleeps: 8 + 1 baby.
Price: €479-€997 (£300-£625).
Bedrooms: 3 doubles, 2 with own shower & wc; 1 room with 2 singles, bunkbeds & sofabed; bathroom & wc.

Booking details:
Oriana Lea
Tel: +44 (0)1264 861178
Fax: +44 (0)1264 861190
E-mail: oj.lea@btinternet.com

Map no: 2

La Grange, La Valette, 50580 Saint Rémy des Landes

Hospitality comes naturally to Jacqueline, the British owner, who bought this 17th-century farmhouse and barn over a decade ago. She is thoroughly integrated into the life of this pretty Norman hamlet and works in the tourist office in nearby Portbail, so is an excellent source of advice on places to go. Her passion is herbs and she's created a special herb garden for the converted barn where you stay. With its delicious views of the orchard and garden, the house has been sympathetically furnished and spotless rooms are generous in comforts and stylish cosiness. Relax after a day on the dunes by the woodburner in the imposing stone fireplace; the living room is full of personal touches and comfy sofas. Downstairs rooms have modern tiled floors and beams, while bedrooms are carpeted and have simple pine furniture and velux windows. Eat out in the garden, take a picnic to the beach three kilometres away, visit the waterside church of Notre-Dame in Portbail and shop at its Tuesday market. *Available Christmas & New Year.*

Sleeps: 4-5.
Price: €399-€669 (£250-£420).
Bedrooms: 1 double with bathroom & wc; 1 twin with shower & wc; sofabed in living room.

Booking details:
Jacqueline Livock
Tel: +33 (0)2 33 07 27 17

Capel, 17 hameau Capel, 50460 Urville Nacqueville

Michel, keen sailor and builder of submarines, wanted a view of the sea; Éliane craved an old house built in traditional Normandy stone. *Et voilà!* this 200-year-old spinner's cottage in a friendly hamlet on the north-west tip of the Cotentin peninsula offered both — and convenience too: the cross-Channel ferry at Cherbourg is just 12km away. One day Michel and Éliane plan to retire here (they currently live nearby) but Michel will happily take you sailing if you ask in advance. Landlubbers and seafarers alike will love the views of the glistening bay from the sheltered south-facing patio; steps lead up to a luxuriant, shrub-filled garden. Inside, the owners have kept the original exposed stone walls, dark old beams and a fine stone fireplace in the living/dining room, although tiled floors are modern and furniture a mix of old and new. Pick your bedroom according to whether you want views of sea or garden. After a day on the beach, eat out on the patio, or in the restaurant 500 metres away.

Sleeps: 5.
Price: €206-€389.
Bedrooms: 1 double; 1 twin; 1 single; shower downstairs; wc.

Booking details:
Michel & Éliane Thomas
Tel: +33 (0)2 33 03 58 16
Fax: +33 (0)2 33 03 58 16

La Mansoiserie, 50760 Anneville en Saire

In the 12th century Barfleur was the busiest port in Normandy; it was here that Henry I's son's ship struck a rock, drowning its royal crew and 100 nobles. The population has been dwindling ever since and today Barfleur is a quiet fishing port on an inlet of the grey granite coast. It's a pleasant place for exploring and shopping (Saturday is market day) while based at La Mansoiserie, a lovely old stone house that stands alone in rolling countryside. Once a store for milk churns from the nearby farm, it's been elegantly furnished by its equally elegant French owner, Madame Feron, who lives three kilometres away. With beams and lovely antiques, rooms are generous in comforts and homely cosiness. There are two sitting rooms and a well-equipped cottage-style kitchen in which to try out some Normandy cuisine. Enjoy the quiet views from the carpeted bedrooms; one has a chic ironwork cot. Walk on the Cotentin peninsula, visit the landing beach of Utah, or discover the museums in Quinéville and Sainte-Marie-du-Mont.

Sleeps: 4 + 1 baby.
Price: €230-€415.
Bedrooms: 1 double plus cot; 1 twin; bathroom; wc.

Booking details:
Bernard & Paulette Feron
Tel: +33 (0)2 33 54 01 28

Map no: 2

La Fèvrerie No 1, 50760 Sainte Geneviève

The owners are a delight: she's charming, bubbly and elegant, he's quieter and full of kindness; together they've grown vegetables on their farm near the sea for as long as they can remember (she was born here). They're now retired and run an idyllic B&B 50 metres down the lane. This creeper-clad 16th-century house was a farm labourer's cottage; the other half is rented out too, and each has its own private front garden where guests can eat out. Madame's passion is interior decoration, and it shows: beams abound, and there are two beautiful antique wooden settees in the large open plan dining/living room. The tiny fishing village of Barfleur is just across the fields, and the invasion beaches a short drive to the south. In summer you can pop over to the nearby island of Tatihou for atmospheric concerts. Don't forget to try the local oysters. *Supplement for cleaning at end of stay.*

Sleeps: 4-5.
Price: €260-€440.
Bedrooms: 1 twin; 1 double with extra single; bathroom; wc.

Booking details:
Marie-France & Maurice Caillet
Tel: +33 (0)2 33 54 33 53
Fax: +33 (0)2 33 22 12 50

La Fèvrerie No 2, 50760 Sainte Geneviève

This creeper-draped semi-detached stone cottage is buffered from the rugged rocky Normandy coast by a swathe of dreamy fields, where Monsieur Caillet's racehorses graze. The owners are a sparkling and cultivated couple whom you would never guess were grandparents. They've now given up vegetable farming and full-time racehorse breeding to run a successful B&B nearby, although Monsieur still breeds a few horses every year. Inside the large living/dining room a great stone fireplace, beams and exposed stone walls provide a warm and welcoming feel. Pretty carpeted bedrooms have dark antique furniture and tranquil views over surrounding fields, and the big double has charming floral pink and green wallpaper. There's a small patio for dining out. Explore the Cotentin peninsula on foot, visit the weekly markets at Barfleur and St Pierre Église, or stroll along the bay in attractive St-Vaast-la-Hougue where Edward III landed on his way to Crécy. Excellent seafood restaurants in Barfleur and Saint-Vaast.

Sleeps: 4-5.
Price: €260-€440.
Bedrooms: 1 double with extra single; 1 twin; shower; wc.

Booking details:
Marie-France & Maurice Caillet
Tel: +33 (0)2 33 54 33 53
Fax: +33 (0)2 33 22 12 50

Map no: 2

Manoir de la Rivière, 14230 Géfosse-Fontenay

Once the watchtower for this medieval fortified farm, you can still see the loopholes through which the guards kept an eye on the enemy. What you'll watch today are the Leharivels' 80-odd dairy cows, which thrive on the lush pasture of the rugged Cotentin peninsula. Isolated at the end of the manor house walled garden, this dolls' house gem is the ultimate lovers' getaway. Arrive in winter and owner Isabelle will have lit a fire for you in the woodburner; come in summer and you'll dine on a sun-drenched terrace before trotting up the outside stone steps to bed. In the bedroom, pristine exposed stone walls, and matching bedcovers and curtains in red and white, create a mood of light and calm. A steep staircase leads down to the tiny beamed living room, just big enough for a sofa to snuggle up in by the fire, and there's a kitchenette in one corner. The beach is a stroll away, and the D-day beaches, including Pointe du Hoc on Omaha beach, where you'll still see German bunkers and shellholes in the cliffs, are nearby. Bliss. *Second gîte in manor house.*

Sleeps: 2.
Price: €213-€297.
Bedrooms: 1 double; shower & wc.

Booking details:
Gérard & Isabelle Leharivel
Tel: +33 (0)2 31 22 64 45
Fax: +33 (0)2 31 22 01 18
E-mail: manoirdelariviere@mageos.com
Web: www.chez.com/manoirdelariviere

Manoir Des Doyens, 14400 Bayeux

If military history is your thing, this 17th-century stone farmhouse is for you. Bayeux, with its famous tapestry, medieval Cathedral and military cemetery, is within walking distance; the Normandy landing beaches are a short drive away; and Lt-Colonel Chilcott, the owner, is a military historian and will take you on a private battlefield tour if you are interested. He and his gentle wife moved here from the Isle of Wight and run a B&B in the main part of the farmhouse (once the property of the Deans of Bayeux, according to the Lt-Colonel). But even if military history isn't for you, you'll love the peace and space of this farm with its grassy courtyard, animals and ancient stone pond. The wing, where you lodge, also has its own walled garden for meals out. Furnishings are basic and somewhat worn, but improve as you ascend: pretty antiques mingle with the modern furniture in the interconnecting gabled bedrooms upstairs. Perfect for a family with children.

Sleeps: 4-6.
Price: €198-€274.
Bedrooms: 1 double with extra single bed, connected to 1 twin; sofabed downstairs; bathroom & wc.

Booking details:
Lt-Col & Mrs Chilcott
Tel: +33 (0)2 31 22 39 09
Fax: +33 (0)2 31 21 97 84
E-mail: chilcott@mail.cpod.fr

Map no: 2

Le Pressoir, Manoir de Laize, 14190 Fontaine-Le-Pin

Apples used to be stored and pressed in this grandiose stone outbuilding to make cider and Calvados. Across the lawns, pretty with blossoming apple trees in the spring, is the 15th-century manor farmhouse, where Tim, Carolyn and their two teenage children live. Country lovers and Francophiles all, they moved from England a decade ago and will enthusiastically advise you on where to eat — and buy the best Calvados. The feel inside the *pressoir* is modern, although ceiling beams have been kept downstairs and a gorgeous white stone fireplace remains in the wooden-floored master bedroom upstairs. Furniture in most rooms is basic, with lots of pine, although you will find some antique beds. Drink in the serene views of lush fields, eat out on the lawn or on your private patio, or join the Knowlmans and their occasional B&B guests for dinner (book in advance). Visit Falaise, the birthplace of William the Conqueror, or cycle or canoe in the gorge of the Orne.

Sleeps: 7 + 1 baby.
Price: €367-€606 (£230-£380).
Bedrooms: 2 twins; 1 double with extra single bed & cot; bathroom & wc.

Booking details:
Tim & Carolyn Knowlman
Tel: +33 (0)2 31 90 23 62
Fax: +33 (0)2 31 90 23 62
E-mail: knowlman@libertysurf.fr

La Maisonnette, Berville, 14170 Saint Pierre sur Dives

These old, old stones were once part of a farmhouse belonging to the Abbey of Saint Pierre sur Dives, whose consecration was attended by William the Conqueror. They've been given a new lease of life by their friendly and hardworking French owner Annick, who retired to this quiet farming hamlet after a career in the hotel industry and now runs a B&B in the other half of this honey-stone house (parts of which date from 1492). Delight in your own private garden, a pond teeming with carp, and serene views over the orchards and fields of the verdant Auge Valley. The inside is simply but pleasingly decorated; there's a big stone fireplace in the living/dining room, and bedrooms on the first and second floors have exposed beams, stone walls and antique bedsteads. If you don't feel like cooking, try some of the *fermes auberges* around; or eat at the Pavé d'Auge restaurant in lovely Beuvron-en-Auge, with its splendid multicoloured half-timbered houses, including the brown and yellow 16th-century Vieux Manoir.

Sleeps: 4-6.
Price: €445-€565.
Bedrooms: 1 double with extra single;
1 attic twin with extra folding bed;
bathroom & wc.

Booking details:
Annick Duhamel
Tel: +33 (0)2 31 20 51 26
Fax: +33 (0)2 31 20 03 03

Map no: 3

Les Saules, Berville, 14170 Saint Pierre sur Dives

This lush corner of the Auge is a cheese-lover's heaven, with Livarot, Camembert and Pont L'Évêque all vying for a place on your cheeseboard. From this lovely stone cottage, right on the *route des fromages*, visit the museum in the château at Livarot (one of the most potent of Normandy cheeses); or in Vimoutiers, learn how Camembert's 'inventor' was taught her techniques by a priest on the run from Brie. Stock up at the unmissable Monday market in Saint Pierre's superb 11th-century market hall and Annick, the French owner, will give you home-grown vegetables and salads to accompany them. This ancient little stone outbuilding was once a chicken house and part of a large farm belonging to the old abbey. Annick runs a B&B in the main house and rents the cottage next door, but here you'll enjoy total privacy with beautiful views of cider apple orchards all around. Comfortable rooms, with exposed stone walls, are traditionally and simply furnished.

Sleeps: 2-4.
Price: €275-€395.
Bedrooms: 2 doubles, 1 downstairs with shower & wc, 1 on mezzanine overlooking living room.

Booking details:
Annick Duhamel
Tel: +33 (0)2 31 20 51 26
Fax: +33 (0)2 31 20 03 03

La Boursaie, Livarot, 14140 Livarot

You can almost smell the intoxicating aroma of fermenting apples as you dine in the groove where the great granite wheel of this old cider press once turned. Apples and cider have made this superb cluster of half-timbered buildings tick since medieval times, and English owner Peter and his German wife Anja have done a remarkable job restoring them, keeping their original character. Ancient cider barrels, wheelbarrows and apple baskets have been used around the grounds, and the interiors of what are now five holiday cottages are decorated with 'ciderabilia' Peter has bought over the years. The large open-plan living/dining room and kitchen have the biggest beams you've ever seen, an attractive terracotta tiled floor, and quaint baroque-style pink velvet armchairs. Bedrooms have seagrass floors, and one is painted shocking raspberry. You won't be alone here, but with 65 acres of land, there's room to roam. Watch the hovering buzzards from your private patch of garden and drink in the fabulous valley views.

Sleeps: 7.
Price: €450-€1,165.
Bedrooms: 2 doubles; 1 twin; 1 single; bathroom; wc; shower & wc downstairs.

Booking details:
Anja & Peter Davies
Tel: +33 (0)2 31 63 14 20
Fax: +33 (0)2 31 63 14 28

Map no: 3

La Grange, Livarot, 14140 Livarot

You'll spot deer in the early mornings, and foxes, badgers and the occasional wild boar roam the magical woods surrounding La Boursaie. The hamlet takes its name from *bource*, the old Norman word for source. Drink in the ancient beauty of this cider farm under the shade of the 300-year-old walnut tree, which towers and protects like a friendly giant. Anja and Peter will bring walnuts, apples and pears to your cottage, and you can buy their home-produced cider and Calvados. La Grange, with its stupendous views over the courtyard, duck pond and lush valley beyond, was formerly the hayloft, and has been attractively converted into a split-level first-floor apartment. Old beams have been skilfully used to divide the flat and blend well with the antique and new pine furniture and seagrass matting. Downstairs Peter has his watercolour studio — you'll spot his work in the cottages — and there's a dining room where the couple, both ex-catering, entertain guests to a weekly feast where you'll taste Norman cooking at its best.

Sleeps: 4.
Price: €450-€830.
Bedrooms: 2 twins, 1 with shower & wc; bathroom & wc.

Booking details:
Anja & Peter Davies
Tel: +33 (0)2 31 63 14 20
Fax: +33 (0)2 31 63 14 28

Le Trou Normand, Livarot, 14140 Livarot

Even the ducks and chickens live in a half-timbered cottage here: no building disrupts the black-and-white beauty of this tranquil farmstead, hidden like a buried treasure in a fold between lush rolling hills. Couples will enjoy this tiny cottage, where once Calvados was distilled, with its long views of apple, cherry and pear orchards. Sit by a comforting fire in the winter and enjoy a glass of home-produced cider. Décor is simple and clean, cream walls are reinforced by deep-red tiled floors and dark-beamed ceilings. You can see the original copper still downstairs, and there's a pretty bedroom under the rafters with attractive blue bedcovers. If you want to walk you can join the *Tour du Pays d'Auge* GR footpath almost at the door, or visit the nearby gardens and Château of Vendeuvre. Camembert is a short drive away, and the cheese's creator, Marie Harel, whose promotion campaign included sending free samples to Napoleon, is commemorated with a statue in the next-door village of Vimoutiers.

Sleeps: 2.
Price: €300-€430.
Bedrooms: 1 double; shower & wc.

Booking details:
Anja & Peter Davies
Tel: +33 (0)2 31 63 14 20
Fax: +33 (0)2 31 63 14 28

Map no: 3

Le Boquet, 14140 Vieux-Pont-en-Auge

Bring walking boots and a hearty appetite: the rich pastures around here produce some of France's best-known cheeses, including Camembert and Pont L'Évêque, and should you over-indulge, there are lovely rolling hills where you can walk it all off. The picture of Norman bliss is completed by this ancient half-timbered farmstead, consisting of a manor house and two farm cottages, which enthusiastic English owner Allison has skilfully converted. Come to enjoy the lush tranquillity of the gardens and the surrounding countryside rather than luxurious furnishings: décor is endearingly old-fashioned, with plenty of patterned rugs and carpets and 'interesting' wallpapers. The homely dining/living room has original beams and some good antique furniture (but no fireplace), while bedrooms have white painted furniture and floral bedcovers and curtains. Allison runs painting and sketching weekends on request. If you want to walk, the GR *Tour du Pays d'Auge* passes nearby; don't miss the stunning 10th-century church in pretty Vieux-Pont-en-Auge.

Sleeps: 4 + 1 baby.
Price: €255-€399 (£160-£250).
Bedrooms: 1 double with cot; 1 twin;
bathroom & wc downstairs.

Booking details:
Allison Nash
Tel: +33 (0)2 31 20 30 62
E-mail: allison_nash@hotmail.com

Ferme de la Pomme, 14590 Le Pin

This red-brick house with its handsome granite roof was once the stables to the farmhouse across the lawns. You'll no longer hear the neighing of horses in here, but they remain the passion of Jocelyne and Philippe; he works at the local stud, and guests are invited to bring their own horses if they wish to ride. The couple have restored and modernised the house with meticulous attention to detail, skilfully blending mellow antique furniture, pretty check fabrics and modern floors and walls. The calming mood is reinforced by pastel-coloured window and picture frames and clean white spaces. The carpeted master bedroom has a feminine, frilly feel, and has stunning views of the lawns and fields outside. You'll share the grounds with the Syllas and their B&B guests, but the sunny paved patio in front is yours alone. Visit the Saturday market in Lisieux for a taste of the marvellous cheeses and ciders for which this lush part of Normandy is famous, or explore its rolling hills and twisting valleys on foot.

Sleeps: 4-5.
Price: €137-€381.
Bedrooms: 1 double; 1 twin with extra rollaway single; shower & wc.

Booking details:
Jocelyne Sylla
Tel: +33 (0)2 31 61 96 09
Fax: +33 (0)2 31 61 96 09
E-mail: cedric.sylla@caramail.com
Web: csylla.multimania.com/gite

Map no: 3

La Vallée Blonde, 27450 Saint Georges-du-Vièvre

You'd almost expect to find Hansel and Gretel at this fairytale half-timbered cottage, hidden in the Normandy woods. The only passers-by will be the cows in the neighbouring fields so if you want to escape completely, this is the place. Peace will be yours as you dine out in your grassy glade under the geraniums, and there are walks galore from your tiny sky-blue front door. The house, once a bakehouse, has been simply furnished by its English owners, who have kept the wooden beams and the original floor tiles and brick and stone skirting. There's a coal-fired stove in the sitting/dining room, and steep stairs lead to a bedroom among the rafters. Because the owners won't be here when you are, you'll be trusted to leave the cottage clean when you leave. Be sure to visit the magical Abbaye de Bec-Hellouin, whose white-robed monks lend a mood of tranquillity to this beautiful valley. Shop in St-Georges-du-Vièvre and visit the Château de Launay with its breathtaking half-timbered Renaissance dovecot. *No washing machine or dishwasher.*

Sleeps: 2.
Price: €287-€438 (£180-£275).
Bedrooms: 1 double; shower & wc downstairs.

Booking details:
Jennifer Murray
Tel: +44 (0)1273 888033
Fax: +44 (0)1273 245855
E-mail: jenmurray@20powis.fsnet.co.uk

Clos Vorin, 27500 Triqueville

This blue and white timbered dolls' house cottage is so pretty, and the idyllic apple orchards in which it stands so lush, you have to pinch yourself to believe it's real. Even when you've crept inside the blue-framed front door, the fairytale continues, with enchanting details like hand-embroidered translucent curtains, colourful beams and, everywhere, clean pure space. This magical cottage is the creation of Eddy and Delphine, who live in the half-timbered house across the garden and who run the village newsagent. Downstairs there's a light and airy living room with lovely pale wooden floors and white walls which perfectly offset the dark antiques (including a piano) and richly coloured hand-woven rugs. Furniture is a successful mix of old and new, expensive and budget, and there's a wonderful baroque-style antique bed in the cosy bedroom upstairs. Drink in the peace of inland Normandy from the hammock suspended between the apple trees. Explore the area's half-timbered houses, walk its meadows and forests, and taste its tempting cheeses, creams and ciders.

Sleeps: 2-4.
Price: €250-€290.
Bedrooms: 1 double; sofabed in living room; shower & wc.

Booking details:
Eddy & Delphine Cayeux
Tel: +33 (0)2 32 56 53 15
Fax: +33 (0)2 32 56 53 15

  Map no: 3

Brittany
Western Loire

Photography by Michael Busselle.

L'Ancien Presbytère, 22420 Tregrom

The scent of climbing roses and honeysuckle greets you as you arrive at this stunning 17th-century grey stone presbytery: Madame's passion is gardening, as you'll see from her colourful borders and you even have a large walled orchard all to yourselves. The house is a wing off the main house where B&B guests lodge, but you have complete privacy. Interior decoration is pretty and personalised — all Madame's handiwork — with plenty of painted wood in smokey hues. There's a lovely kitchen with blue-painted cupboards, waxed terracotta floor and sunny yellow wallpapered walls. Bedrooms, on the first and attic floors, are in old-fashioned pastels with matching floral curtains and bedspreads, unusual canework beds and antique painted wardrobes, and soothing garden views. Buy your morning croissants at the organic baker's behind the house; for other provisions there are local weekly markets. It may take time to get to know Madame, but once you've broken the ice she's a fountain of knowledge, and will advise on beaches and châteaux to visit.

Sleeps: 6.
Price: €560.
Bedrooms: 2 twins, 2 singles; bathroom & wc on ground floor; shower & wc on second floor.

Booking details:
Nicole de Morchoven
Tel: +33 (0)2 96 47 94 15
Fax: +33 (0)2 96 47 94 15

Map no: 1

Château de Bonabry, 22120 Hillion

This little gem used to house the archives of the château (built by the Viscomte's ancestors in 1373): the family discovered piles of musty parchment documents when they restored it a few years ago. With the sea at the end of the drive, your own rose and shrub-filled walled garden to spill out into in the summer, and two very likeable and lively hosts, this is a wonderful place for a small family to stay. Downstairs rooms have stone vaulted ceilings, crimson-washed walls and ancient terracotta tile floors. Furnishings are simple but adequate. Bedrooms, enthusiastically restored by the Viscomtesse, have beams and polished wooden floors. There's a double with a canopied bed and yellow fabric-clad walls, and a twin in pretty pinks and whites. If they are not out riding, your hosts will be on hand to help if you need them, and the Viscomte may bring offerings from his personal vegetable garden. *The château also sleeps up to 11 B&B guests.*

Sleeps: 4.
Price: €460-€915.
Bedrooms: 1 double; 1 twin; shower & wc.

Booking details:
Vicomte & Vicomtesse du Fou de Kerdaniel
Tel: +33 (0)2 96 32 21 06
Fax: +33 (0)2 96 32 21 06

Map no: 1

Ti Vilamo, Créhal, 56590 Ile de Groix

This is the kind of home your granny might have lived in: old-fashioned, lacey and full of memories. Sandwiched between its neighbours and hidden behind a wall, the exterior of this dolls' house cottage is unassuming but inside it has the warmth and authenticity of a family home. Ancient clocks chime on the hour, there's an antique dresser full of assorted crockery and a great stone fireplace. The small kitchen has floral red and green wall tiles, a salmon pink floor and green stained wooden cupboard doors. Cosy bedrooms have sloping pine-panelled ceilings, an assortment of wallpapers and more lace and frills. This tiny eight kilometre-long rocky island, reached by ferry (45 minutes) from Lorient, is a nature lover's delight: you can walk 25km around its coast, there's good bird-watching in the nature reserve, and good cycle paths. Find sandy beaches near the dauntingly-named Pointe de l'Enfer (Hell's Point) and on the east coast.

Sleeps: 4.
Price: €427-€587.
Bedrooms: 1 double; 1 twin; shower room downstairs; wc; wc upstairs.

Booking details:
Christiane Villamaux
Tel: +33 (0)2 35 96 10 15
Fax: +33 (0)2 35 96 75 25
E-mail: christiane.villamaux@libertysurf.fr
Web: tivilamo.ifrance.com

Map no: 1

Château de Coët Caret, 44410 Herbignac

Come here for a taste of life in a genuine French château (Monsieur's family has lived on this estate since the 15th century) for glorious views over 100 hectares of parkland where horses gently graze, and for access to fine beaches and birdwatching. The apartment, on the second floor of the château, is basic: don't expect Louis XVI furniture — but there are a few antiques in heavy oak, and generous windows provide fine views of the grounds. Floors are wooden except in the bedrooms, which are carpeted, and the living room has vinyl wallpaper. In contrast to the large and airy bedrooms is the tiny, functional, modernised fitted kitchen, with orange walls and a terracotta tile floor. Listen to the crickets and the birds from your splendid canopied double bed, or wallow in the *sabot*-style bath next door. If you don't want to cook, join B&B guests for dinner in true aristocratic style downstairs. There's excellent birdwatching in La Grande Brière marshlands nature reserve, and the ancient walled town of Guérande is fascinating to visit.

Sleeps: 4-5.
Price: €292-€494.
Bedrooms: 1 double with extra single bed; 1 twin; 1 bathroom & wc.

Booking details:
François & Cécile de la Monneraye
Tel: +33 (0)2 40 91 41 20
Fax: +33 (0)2 40 91 37 46
E-mail: coetcaret@multimania.com
Web: www.welcome.to/coetcaret.com

Map no: 2

Le Vieux Coët Caret, 44410 Herbignac

Experience the life of the French country aristocracy: the de la Monneraye family have lived on this gorgeous estate since the 15th century, and this lovely stone building was part of the manor house before the château was built. Get a glimpse inside the château by joining your formal but charming and hospitable hosts for dinner. You'll be expected to dress accordingly and to mingle with B&B guests and visitors occupying the self-catering apartment (and children will need to be on best behaviour!) but it's an unmissable occasion. On other evenings dine out in your beautiful secluded garden after a day's riding in the grounds (ask Madame for details) or a trip to the beach. Inside, the house is simply but pleasantly furnished, with antiques, stone floors and beamed ceilings downstairs, and matching floral fabrics and fitted brown carpets in the bedrooms upstairs. The kitchen, which opens onto the lawn, has attractive quarry tiles and ancient beams. Come here for peace, birdsong and a whiff of history.

Sleeps: 4.
Price: €353-€631.
Bedrooms: 1 double; 1 twin; sofabed (to be used with permission only); shared shower & wc.

Booking details:
François & Cécile de la Monneraye
Tel: +33 (0)2 40 91 41 20
Fax: +33 (0)2 40 91 37 46
E-mail: coetcaret@multimania.com
Web: www.welcome.to/coetcaret.com

Map no: 2

Le Relais de La Rinière, 44430 Le Landreau

You're surrounded by vines: this is Muscadet country and the clay soils of the area produce some particularly ambitious wines. Indulge in some private tastings in the huge garden — a cocktail of wisteria, lawns and colourful surprises — or pop off to one of the nearby *caves* to meet some local *vignerons*. You'll enjoy your delightful hosts Françoise and Louis, who run a B&B in the imposing coaching inn (of which your cottage is an outhouse). He used to be a baker, she's a keen jam-maker, and they moved here from Normandy bringing some lovely antiques with them. A fine old dresser and *armoire* house the pretty crockery in the light and sunny dining/living room/kitchen and there's an old oak table for family gatherings. Colour schemes are adventurous: ochre-sponged walls downstairs, and, in the bedrooms, low ceiling beams painted bright purple. One room has an old bread oven. Discover historic Nantes, with its splendid 18th-century houses and its château, or visit the slick wine museum at Le Pallet. There's great cycling too.

Sleeps: 5.
Price: €220-€495.
Bedrooms: 1 double; 1 triple; shower & wc.

Booking details:
Françoise & Louis Lebarillier
Tel: +33 (0)2 40 06 41 44
Fax: +33 (0)2 51 13 10 52
E-mail: riniere@netcourrier.com
Web: www.riniere.com

Map no: 2

43

La Gaubertiere, 49310 Saint Paul du Bois

History oozes from every crevice of this magical 15th-century tower. The Ricour family have lived in the half-moated manor house next door for the past one and a half centuries, and during the war German soldiers were billeted here (you'll spot their sword slash marks on the family portraits in the traditional, ever-so-French *salon*). When she's not doting on visiting grandchildren, Madame, vivacious and warm, teaches upholstery and lodges B&B guests. Bedrooms are on four storeys, so choose your view: there's a low-beamed twin on the ground floor, a master double with bird of paradise design fabrics and pretty antiques on the first, and twins on the second and third, reached by a narrow spiral staircase. Carry out your ablutions in a tiny turret at the back of the tower with oval windows looking down onto the large, well-established gardens. Eat outside when it's warm and absorb the deep peace of this wonderful estate. There's a grocer, baker and a museum of theatrical costume in the village, two kilometres away.

Sleeps: 6-8.
Price: €457-€762. (Electricity supp. November-March.)
Bedrooms: 1 double; 3 twins; 1 bathroom; 2 wcs.

Booking details:
Beatrice Ricour
Tel: +33 (0)2 41 75 81 87

Map no: 2

La Chalopinière, 49150 Le Vieil Baugé

Your dining room is the shade of the huge weeping willow in front of the house; if you play your cards right Jill, the English owner, will hang a candelabra there so you can talk well into the summer nights over a bottle of Anjou. There's a friendly family atmosphere here: if you wish, you can mingle with chickens, cats and ponies, Jill and Mike's two children and up to six B&B guests. If you want total privacy, however, you can have that too: your first-floor apartment in the extension to the 15th-century farmhouse is totally self-contained, reached by its own (steep) outside staircase. Inside, the mood is minimalist, with dark exposed roof beams and country furniture set off by spotless white walls. The floors are parquet throughout and there's a woodburner in the living/dining room/kitchen. Jill, lively and fun, will cook you dinner if you ask in advance, and will drop eggs, wine and garden vegetables by your door. The bustling market town of Baugé, with good restaurants and a weekly market, is less than five kilometres away.

Sleeps: 4.
Price: €320-€480.
Bedrooms: 1 double; 1 twin;
bathroom & wc.

Booking details:
Michael & Jill Coyle
Tel: +33 (0)2 41 89 04 38
Fax: +33 (0)2 41 89 04 38
E-mail: rigbycoyle@aol.com

Map no: 7

Le Haut Joreau, 49350 Gennes

One guest called it the Hens' Paradise. All that remains to show that this beautifully restored house was once a hen-house are the nesting boxes, now used for storing pans in the kitchen/dining room. The hen-house was once part of the estate of the château next door, and Jean-Baptiste, an architect, spotted it and fell in love with it while surveying the château. He and his energetic and elegant wife, Annick, have decorated well: the cool sitting room with its waxed terracotta tiled floor, stone walls and woodburner, is simply and beautifully furnished in autumn colours. A spiral staircase leads to unfussy, comfortable bedrooms. Barely a kilometre from the pretty Loire-side town of Gennes, the house stands at the bottom of a secluded valley with steep wooded slopes where deer and wild boar roam. A stream separates the garden from a meadow where sheep and an aged horse peacefully graze. If you can raise yourself from your deckchair on the terrace, there's boating on the Loire, troglodyte villages and some lesser-known châteaux to explore, and interesting wines to taste.

Sleeps: 5.
Price: €300-€380.
Bedrooms: 2 twins, 1 with extra single; shared bathroom & wc.

Booking details:
Annick & Jean-Baptiste Boisset
Tel: +33 (0)2 41 38 02 58
Fax: +33 (0)2 41 38 15 02
E-mail: joreau@fr.st
Web: www.joreau.fr.st

Map no: 7

Le Manoir de Champfreau, 49730 Varennes sur Loire

There's something gloriously outrageous about this gleaming white 15th-century manor house, once a fortified farm. The kitchen has black tiles and pewter plates, and there's a 'four-poster' bath, with splendid ball and claw feet. Once you've wallowed in it, sink into a four-poster bed decked in luxurious heavy fabrics and wake up to views of the topiaries in the courtyard. "More than once the house has shown that bricks, stone and cement can only be pushed so far before it says 'No more'", reads the brochure. History oozes from every crevice here: family portraits and tapestries hang from the thick sandstone walls, and solid antique furniture and coats-of-arms recall the manor's former aristocratic inhabitants. Michel, the kind and unobtrusive manager, lives in a converted outhouse and is on hand if you need advice. In the heart of the UNESCO-designated heritage site of the Loire, and near the confluence of the Loire and the Vienne rivers, you're in the perfect spot for visiting some of the finest châteaux, including Saumur, Montsoreau and Chinon.

Sleeps: 6.
Price: €640-€885.
Bedrooms: 1 double with ensuite shower/wc; 2 doubles; 1 bathroom.

Booking details:
Michel Rondeau
Tel: +33 (0)2 41 51 47 95
E-mail: m.rondeau@wanadoo.fr

Château de Montaupin, 72330 Oizé

Everything is round in this unusual stone *pigeonnier* in the gardens of an ever-so-French 18th-century château. Furnishings are functional rather than luxurious, but you'll come to enjoy the peaceful setting among woods and fields and, if you choose it, the warm company of your young and friendly French hosts. You can join Laurent and Marie and their B&B guests for dinner in the château if you ask in advance; and they'll advise on places to visit. The ground floor of the *pigeonnier* has a compact kitchen — curved of course — and a pretty living room with old terracotta tiles laid in wooden-framed squares. The pleasant first-floor bedroom has attractive fabrics and tranquil views; children will be snugly content on the top floor under the conical roof. You can dine in the château garden where there's also a barbecue, or try a game of boules, or take a dip in the shared heated pool. There's a great auberge nearby if you don't feel like cooking. Book well in advance if you're here for the car racing in Le Mans.

Sleeps: 4-6.
Price: €228-€457.
Bedrooms: 1 double on first floor;
1 four-bed room on second floor;
shower & wc on ground floor.

Booking details:
Laurent Senechal & Marie David
Tel: +33 (0)2 43 87 81 70
Fax: +33 (0)2 43 87 26 25
E-mail: chateaudemontaupin@oreka.com

Map no: 7

Le Four de Villeprouvé, 53170 Ruille Froid Fonds

Here is bucolic peace, oodles of history, and a cranny-filled cottage as full of colourful stories and character as its wonderful owners. It used to be the grain store for the monks who lived in the priory nearby (now a farm and B&B run by Christophe and Christine). Alongside raising cattle and children and caring for guests, they've miraculously found time to lavish care and attention on this exquisite stone house: she sewed pretty drapes for the four-poster bed; he crafted the new staircase within the old frame; both have carefully kept original features such as old beams, the bread oven and a *moru* chest, traditionally used to move a family's worldly belongings around the country. In the living room you'll even find an ancient settle against the wall, inside the seat of which hens, living outside, used to lay eggs which their owners would find in time for breakfast. Furniture is antique, views are idyllic, and you can sample Christine's wholesome cooking if the B&B is not full — just ask in advance.

Sleeps: 6-8
Price: €239-€367 (£150-£230).
Bedrooms: 4 doubles (1 with four-poster & steep ladder to double bed on mezzanine); bathroom & wc; wc.

Booking details:
Christine Davenel
Tel: +33 (0)2 43 07 71 62
Fax: +33 (0)2 43 07 71 62

Loire Valley
Poitou – Charentes
Limousin

Photography by Michael Busselle.

Les Genêts, 18200 Nozières

Compact, stylish and tranquil: this charming stone farm cottage looks like something out of *Alice in Wonderland*. Roses decorate the pale stone front, a great vine drapes over the pergola and in the fields all around Charolais cows gently munch. The house is far larger than it looks from the outside: rooms are light and airy, and are furnished simply but with flair. Marie-Claude, the delightful, elegant owner who lives in the farmhouse a kilometre away, has thought through every detail, from moon and star cut-outs in the bedroom shutters to tartan bows on the picture hooks. Downstairs, tiled floors and whitewashed walls give a homely, country feel. The living room has friendly sofas with tartan throws and you can still see the old bread oven in the dining room fireplace. The two bedrooms have pine floorboards, antique beds and pretty fabrics. The kitchen leads into the grassy garden and you can eat on the patio in the front. There's good cycling around and a Saturday market in Saint Amand. A real gem.

Sleeps: 4.
Price: €300-€365.
Bedrooms: 2 twins each with basin; wc; shower & wc downstairs.

Booking details:
Marie-Claude Dussert
Tel: +33 (0)2 48 96 47 45
Fax: +33 (0)2 48 96 07 71

Map no: 8

Lavande, Le Grand Ajoux, 36370 Chalais

One family comes here every year to watch the dragonflies hatch on the estate's two lakes. On the southern edge of the Brenne National Park (famous for its thousand lakes), and in 53 hectares of private parkland, the place is a paradise for birdwatchers and nature-lovers. Lavande is one of two stables which have been elegantly converted by the equally elegant and energetic Madame Jonquière-Aymé, who runs a B&B in the handsome manor house next door. At opposite ends of the lavender-fringed pool, each cottage has a private patio for sunbathing or dining. Inside, cheerful sky-blue chairs and soft furnishings contrast sympathetically with the exposed stone walls, stripped ceiling beams and lovely terracotta tile floor, with old and new pieces of furniture sitting happily side by side. Enjoy views of the family's horses and donkeys grazing the paddocks from the pretty little downstairs bedroom. There are plenty of walks from the house, and Georges Sand fans can drive to the Vallée Noire, where she lived, and visit the museum at La Châtre.

Sleeps: 2-4.
Price: €275-€535.
Bedrooms: 1 double; 1 double sofabed in living room; shower & wc.

Booking details:
Aude de la Jonquière-Aymé
Tel: +33 (0)2 54 37 72 92
Fax: +33 (0)2 54 37 56 60
E-mail: grandajoux@aol.com
Web: members.aol.com/grandajoux

Map no: 7

Amande, Le Grand Ajoux, 36370 Chalais

Fifty-three hectares of parkland are yours to roam, and if you're interested Madame will whisk you off on deer and wild boar spotting trips. Alternatively fish in the private lake (bring your own rod), or simply unwind by the pool a few steps from your pretty blue bedroom door. Elegantly cosy, this tiny, 300-year-old converted stable has been imaginatively restored while keeping original stone walls and tiled floors. Sit by the stone fireplace on cool evenings while you plan the next day's activities, and listen out for owls while you sleep in the ground-floor bedroom. Steep pine stairs lead to a small mezzanine twin bedroom for children. Visit the Abbey of St-Savin with its 13th-century frescoes of the hermit Saint Savinus, and the Loire châteaux, 90 minutes' drive away. There are interesting wines to taste if you're an *aficionado*: try Vouvray and Chinon from the Touraine; film buffs may prefer the Cuvée Cyrano, produced by the Château of Tigné, which is owned by actor Gérard Dépardieu.

Sleeps: 2-4.
Price: €245-€535.
Bedrooms: 1 double; 1 twin on mezzanine; shower & wc.

Booking details:
Aude de la Jonquière-Aymé
Tel: +33 (0)2 54 37 72 92
Fax: +33 (0)2 54 37 56 60
E-mail: grandajoux@aol.com
Web: members.aol.com/grandajoux

La Maison Rose, 37460 Loché-sur-Indrois

Slip through the little blue door in the wall and you could be in Hodgson Burnett's *The Secret Garden*. With its gorgeous pink roses and creeper-clad stone walls, the private courtyard garden in which this 18th-century farm cottage stands is truly magical. Sit out among the lavender bushes and absorb the deep peace and promise of this pretty village on the poplar-lined banks of the Indrois river. Inside the house is no less bewitching, its colourful furnishings and old oak beams exuding warmth and well-being. James, the English owner, teaches art and design, and whitewashed walls are hung with his paintings in bright primary colours. Enjoy views of the river from the two double bedrooms: one is reached via a twin. Artists will celebrate the famous Touraine light, children will enjoy exploring the fields and woods beyond the house and you'll love Loches, with its medieval citadel, blue slate roofs and twice-weekly market. There are great walks along the river valley too. *Tennis in the village. Discount for fortnightly bookings.*

Sleeps: 4-6.
Price: €422-€677 (£265-£425).
Bedrooms: 2 doubles; 1 twin; shower & wc; bathroom.

Booking details:
Flora & James Cockburn
Tel: +44 (0)1732 357022 or
+33 (0)2 47 92 61 79 (school holidays)
E-mail: mrsfscockburn@aol.com
Web: www.lamaisonrose.com

Oysters, 8 Coulangé, 37460 Villeloin-Coulangé

Tranquillity is yours in this Loire hamlet, so small that there aren't any streets, and houses just have numbers. To shop you have the treat of going to Montrésor: a veritable treasure, as its name suggests, with its lovely château dominating a jumble of village houses. Visit the *boulangerie*, whose bread is justly famous. The 200-year-old stone farmhouse, which can be rented as one house or as two self-contained cottages, has been attractively refurbished by its lively and friendly owners, Janet and Edo, who live across the courtyard. The house had been unoccupied for 10 years when they bought it, so restoring it was a labour of love. Supposedly retired — Janet from being a full-time mum, Edo from working as a barrister — they say they've never worked so hard. Spotless interiors are a feast of colourful patterned rugs, high-quality furniture and old oak beams. Downstairs, the smaller cottage (for two to three), is decorated in sunny yellows while the larger house (for four to five), has a beige, red and gold colour scheme. *Art courses available in Montrésor. Shop in Villeloin.*

Sleeps: 6 + 1 baby.
Price: €620-€995.
Bedrooms: 1 double/twin; 1 double; 1 twin; 2 showers; 2 wcs. Camp beds on request.

Booking details:
Janet & Edo de Vries
Tel: +33 (0)2 47 92 64 05
Fax: +33 (0)2 47 92 64 97
E-mail: edo_de_vries@hotmail.com
Web: www.stayatoysters.com

Moulin de la Follaine, 37310 Azay sur Indre

The servants who worked in the medieval mill opposite lived here and Danie will show you the old Azay flour sacks if you wish. Your young and friendly hosts run a B&B in the millhouse, but you have your own patio (with barbecue) and garden too, so there's perfect privacy and peace. Your kitchen/living room is pleasantly decorated with a comfortable mix of modern and antique country furniture and a stone fireplace; bedrooms are uncluttered too, with white walls and friezes that give an original touch. There's masses to do here, from cycling to ping-pong to fishing, with tackle supplied, or enjoy the colourful gardens, rushing waterways and lake with ornamental geese. You'll love the weekly markets in Azay and Loches (worth visiting for its castle and dungeon, too) but if you prefer not to cook there's a wonderful auberge a stroll away that specialises in traditional regional cooking. *Unguarded water makes the house unsuitable for young children.*

Sleeps: 6.
Price: €375-€450.
Bedrooms: 2 doubles with extra single beds; bathroom & wc.

Booking details:
Danie Lignelet
Tel: +33 (0)2 47 92 57 91
Fax: +33 (0)2 47 92 57 91
E-mail: moulindelafollaine@wanadoo.fr
Web: www.multimania.com/moulindefollaine

Map no: 7

Les Petites Ouldes, 37150 Francueil

A short stroll from the Loire's glittering prize, the Château de Chenonceau, and in five acres of landscaped grounds, this ground-floor apartment in the wing of a manor house exudes elegance and style. Its large light rooms and orangery-style arched French windows have a Mediterranean feel, reinforced by the pretty cane furniture, sunny fabrics and terracotta floors. The house has been restored over two decades by English owner Valerie, as elegant and charming as her houses, who lives in the red-brick manor. Valerie treats guests as friends — while also being discreet — and will leave a bottle of the estate's own Sauvignon in your fridge for your arrival and will cook you a gourmet dinner using home-grown produce, if you ask in advance. Within the high-ceilinged bedroom there are vases of fresh flowers and luxurious linen; without, views of manicured lawns and topiaries and a private walled terrace. If you ever tire of drinking in the tranquillity of this beautiful place, there's a scenic four-hour walk from Saint-Martin-le-Beau to Chenonceau.

Sleeps: 2.
Price: €575-€690.
Bedrooms: 1 double; bathroom & wc.

Booking details:
Valerie Faccini
Tel: +33 (0)2 47 23 95 07
Fax: +33 (0)2 47 23 82 90
E-mail: faccini@freesurf.fr
Web: www.lespetitesouldes.free.fr

Le Four de Boulanger, Rue de la cour, 79190 Mandegault

With its sunflower fields, honey stone walls and carthorses, the tiny village of Mandegault reminds you how rural France used to be. Life slows to a deliciously tranquil pace, a pace which English owners Alison and Francis have been careful to respect at their 18th-century farmstead. Hens and ducks potter in the courtyard (children are invited to help collect the eggs at feeding time), sheep graze in the fields, and the wonderfully fertile soil produces everything from cherries to famous Charentais melons. The couple have been equally respectful of local styles and materials in the conversion of the bakery and the stables, both rented out as cottages. In the bakery, the original vaulted stone bread oven and authentic diamond-shaped *œil de bœuf* windows have been kept. Inside, natural fabrics, oak beams and stone walls create a mood of soothing elegance. In the main bedroom, pretty red stencilling on the floorboards and curtains give a dash of colour to the splendid carved wooden bed and matching wardrobe painted in cream.

Sleeps: 4-6.
Price: €303-€526 (£190-£330).
Bedrooms: 1 double; 1 twin; sofabed in living room; bathroom & wc downstairs.

Booking details:
Francis & Alison Hudson
Tel: +33 (0)5 49 29 65 31
E-mail: fabjhudson@aol.com

Map no: 7

Les Écuries, Rue de la Cour, 79190 Mandegault

Enjoy a glass of chilled *Pineau de Charentes*, the wickedly delicious local aperitif, under the wisteria-clad pergola of these pretty stone stables. Alison and Francis, both artists and ex-teachers of art and technology, have put their talents to good use, carefully furnishing and decorating the ground-floor cottage. The result is pure rustic charm. As in the old bakery next door, natural colours and fabrics predominate and rooms have exposed honey-coloured stone walls and oak beams. Spotless bedrooms are simple yet elegant, with scrubbed wooden floorboards and antique iron or wooden beds. Pick herbs from your garden and eat them with fresh organic vegetables which the Hudsons will supply. The garden is private, but can interconnect with the garden next door if two families rent the two cottages together. Chef Boutonne, the nearest town, has a fairytale château, fascinating ancient *lavoirs* (washhouses) and a lively weekly market. *Children can use the large paddling pool.*

Sleeps: 4.
Price: €271-€462 (£170-£290).
Bedrooms: 1 double; 1 twin; shower & wc.

Booking details:
Francis & Alison Hudson
Tel: +33 (0)5 49 29 65 31
E-mail: fabjhudson@aol.com

Les Ecots, 86460 Availles Limousine

This 380-acre sheep farm has been in Pierre's family for generations and 15 years ago Pierre and Line moved back here (from New Zealand) to run it organically. The dynamic couple adore children — they've two of their own — and Pierre is more than happy to take youngsters out on his quad bike and trailer to check on his flock. Line, gentle and smiling, makes wonderful jams when she's not cooking for B&B guests and will leave you a pot to greet you. The cottage, at one end of the long farmhouse in the old grainstore, has its own garden with swings and a covered patio (with ancient bread oven) where you can eat out. You're also free to roam the farm if you wish. Inside, walls are of exposed stone and furniture is mainly modern, although old artefacts have been kept, like the butterchurn in the sitting room. The three bedrooms are cosy and comfortable without being lavish. There's lots to do in the area, from cycling and walking to visiting Poitiers. Ideal for families who enjoy farm life. *Meals available with B&B guests in main house on request.*

Sleeps: 5-6.
Price: €230-€305.
Bedrooms: 1 twin; 2 doubles; shower with wc upstairs; wc downstairs.

Booking details:
Pierre & Line Salvaudon
Tel: +33 (0)5 49 48 59 17
Fax: +33 (0)5 49 48 59 17

 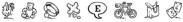

Chataignier, La Boulinière, 86290 La Trimouille

Antiques and interior decoration are Deby's passion (she owns an antique shop in England), and furnishings throughout this lovely converted barn bear the stamp of her elegant eye. If you think the house looks familiar it might be because you've seen it in an interiors magazine — it's featured in several. Furnished with locally-bought antiques, these spotless rooms are a serene symphony of fabrics, textures and colours. The living/dining room, vast and light, has wonderful exposed beamed ceilings and welcoming flame-coloured sofas; French windows lead to the pool (yours alone) and gardens, where you can listen to the birdsong for which this area, near the Brenne National Park, is famous. The splendid master bedroom, complete with grand brass bed and luxurious linen, has its own sitting room and bathroom. Deby raises a family and runs a B&B in the family home next door, and will advise you on local markets. There's great walking: the GR48 footpath runs right past the front door. *Winter lets for two to four at reduced rates.*

Sleeps: 10.
Price: €690-€2,060.
Bedrooms: 3 doubles, 2 with own bathroom & wc; 2 twins; 1 bathroom & wc.

Booking details:
Richard & Deby Earls
Tel: +33 (0)5 49 91 55 88
Fax: +33 (0)5 49 91 02 70
E-mail: la-bouliniere@interpc.fr
Web: www.interpc.fr/jr-earls/bbweb.htm

The Cottage, La Grande Metairie, 86220 Leugny

The stuff of dreams! Rose was bewitched by La Grande Metairie which she thought looked like an illustration by Arthur Rackham. Ten years and 200 rose bushes on, this ancient farm with views over the Creuse valley keeps its enchantment. The stone farm buildings with their unusually sloping roofs surround a courtyard, shaded by fruit trees; under one stands a life-size effigy of your opera singer host Richard. This fun and cultured couple are often there to help if you need them. The inside of the cottage will cast its spell over you too: friendly old armchairs around a woodburner in the cool kitchen/living room, and everywhere dark, gnarled beams. Upstairs there are ancient iron bedsteads (with modern mattresses) and gabled beamed ceilings. Dine out on a private terrace in the large dreamy garden, jump into the (shared) pool surrounded by roses, or treat yourself to tennis. *Let with studio first fortnight July and last week Aug (£900). Let with studio and owners' house, sleeping total of 16, for six weeks from mid-July. Prices on request.*

Sleeps: 4-5.
Price: €511-€670 (£320-420).
Bedrooms: 1 double with bathroom & wc; 1 twin; bathroom & wc; 1 single on landing.

Booking details:
Richard & Rose Angas
Tel: +44 (0)208 743 1745
Fax: +44 (0)208 743 1745
E-mail: angas@freeuk.com

Map no: 7

The Studio, La Grande Metairie, 86220 Leugny

There's wood everywhere in this little jewel-among-the-rafters in the old farm stables. Stripped age-worn beams form the sloping ceilings and there are hefty old boards on the floor. A large iron-framed double bed is screened from the living/kitchen area by pretty Indian-print curtains, and similar fabrics cover a sofabed. You look onto the grassy courtyard on one side and onto the Creuse valley and the tennis court on the other. Stone steps lead down to a private terrace and garden. Come here to relax in the company (when they're there) of your interesting hosts, Rose and Richard, and to explore an unspoiled area of France. Once you've roamed the property's three acres of gardens and woodland, there are châteaux to visit, restaurants and wines to sample, and pleasant walks and cycle rides. A baker delivers daily, and you can buy fresh eggs, goat's cheese and honey from the local farm. *Baby-sitting available. Studio and cottage let together first fortnight July and last week Aug. Let with cottage and owners' house for six weeks from mid-July.*

Sleeps: 2-3.
Price: €319-€415 (£200-£260).
Bedrooms: 1 double; sofabed; shower & wc.

Booking details:
Richard & Rose Angas
Tel: +44 (0)208 743 1745
Fax: +44 (0)208 743 1745
E-mail: angas@freeuk.com

9 clos des gouverneurs, St-Martin, 17410 Ile de Ré

You're likely to spot film stars and politicians strolling the streets of this pretty fishing port whose whitewashed houses cluster around the stone quays of a well-protected harbour. The Ile de Ré, with its 30km of sandy beaches, pine forests and good taste, is a place people return to year after year — with good reason. This old green-shuttered ground-floor apartment in a quiet side street is a great spot from which to explore St-Martin's narrow cobbled streetsw relax in harbour-side cafés, and watch flat-bottomed oyster boats arriving with their catch. You can investigate the island by bike (a cycleway goes all the way round) and there's excellent birdwatching in the salt marshes. The apartment has been superbly restored by its (absent) English owners. In the light living room/kitchen beautiful terracotta tiles and a couple of antique pieces of furniture contrast with the pure white ceiling and clean exposed stone walls. Bedrooms have a modern feel, and there are two tiny patios, one with an old well, where you can eat.

Sleeps: 4.
Price: €407-€574 (£255-£360).
Bedrooms: 1 double; 1 room with bunkbeds; shower; wc.

Booking details:
Elspeth Charlton & Graham d'Albert
Tel: +33 (0)5 46 33 60 88

Map no: 11

Le Donjon, Château de Crazannes, 17350 Crazannes

Follow in the steps of the Black Prince who stayed in the original castle in 1362. The owner is a descendent of the Marshall of France who finally defeated him — but only discovered the link after buying the château 25 years ago. The *donjon*, or keep, where you'll be staying, is one of the oldest remaining parts of the castle, now listed as a *Monument Historique*, and has twisting stone staircases, crenellations and magical views over the 16-acre estate. Absorb the fascinating history among surroundings both utterly peaceful and unashamedly luxurious: furniture is antique, maids will clean daily, you share a heated swimming pool with B&B guests staying in the château, and you can even hire a cook if you wish. Eat out on the terrace or in the large dining room, with exposed stone walls, a grand fireplace, and beautiful waxed terracotta tiled floors. Wind your way up to the elegantly simple bedrooms, all with dreamy views of the castle and the moat, and on upwards to a study and terrace in the clouds. Unique.

Sleeps: 6.
Price: €1,375-€2,285.
Bedrooms: 3 doubles, each with
bathroom & wc.

Booking details:
Herve de Rochefort
Tel: +33 (0)6 80 65 40 96
Fax: +33 (0)5 46 91 34 46
E-mail: crazannes@worldonline.fr
Web: www.crazannes.com

Le Manoir, Manoir Souhait, 17490 Gourvillette

The name means 'wish' and you might well make one to come here. The majestic arched Charentais porchway promises something grand, and you won't be disappointed: a stunning 17th-century manor house with its own enclosed garden, original washhouse and *pigeonnier*. Liz and Will, a young and energetic British couple who live next door, have researched the manor's origins meticulously and will, if you're interested, show you the coats of arms of the Merveilleux family, who built the house in 1620. There's a homely kitchen with a terracotta tiled floor and a massive table and in summer you can spill out onto the patio. An amazing glass-and-brass staircase takes you to bedrooms decorated with a successful mix of antique and modern furniture. There's plenty to do here: the coast and La Rochelle are only an hour's drive; you can visit the distilleries in nearby Cognac; or relax by the pool, shared with guests from the neighbouring cottage. For large family gatherings it's perfect.

Sleeps: 14 + 1 baby.
Price: €1,095-€2,590.
Bedrooms: 3 doubles; 1 double plus single; 1 single; 2 twins; shower & wc; 2 bathrooms & wcs.

Booking details:
Will & Liz Weeks
Tel: +33 (0)5 46 26 18 41
Fax: +33 (0)5 46 24 64 68
E-mail: willweeks@aol.com

Map no: 11

Le Verger, Manoir Souhait, 17490 Gourvillette

You can still see the stone oven in the dining room on which the house's former inhabitants cooked their pigeons. The birds, a delicacy reserved for the gentry, were reared in the *pigeonnier*, just outside the gates. In the tiny village of Gourvillette, the house is in the grounds of the 17th-century *manoir* which is also rented out by British owners Liz and Will. Camaraderie between the two houses is encouraged: guests at both are invited to an aperitif on the day they arrive, and you'll get to know each other by the pool. The interior is light and clean and the furniture mostly modern pine, although ancient roof beams have been kept. Le Verger used to house farmworkers who made cognac, and in the pretty village of Cognac (only 20 minutes' drive away) you can go on tours of the distilleries of names like Remy Martin, Hennessy and Courvoisier. Try the area's other tipple too, *Pineau de Charentes*, a sweet aperitif. If you feel active, bikes can be hired locally and there are lovely rides and walks.

Sleeps: 4-5.
Price: €564-€1,129.
Bedrooms: 1 double plus single;
1 twin; shared bathroom & wc.

Booking details:
Will & Liz Weeks
Tel: +33 (0)5 46 26 18 41
Fax: +33 (0)5 46 24 64 68
E-mail: willweeks@aol.com

Map no: 11

La Maison de la Fontaine, 17490 Gourvillette

On vit au rhythme du vieillissement du cognac ("We live at the speed that cognac ages") is the local saying, and it sums up well the lazy pace of life in this wealthy cognac-producers' village. Unwind completely in this typical Charentais mansion, built, like many houses here, at the end of the 19th century when Cognac was in its heyday, and before phylloxera decimated the area's vineyards. Proud and grand, behind green wrought-iron gates and high sand-coloured stone walls, the three-storey house has been attractively restored by its English owners. In contrast to the formal exterior, rooms downstairs are relaxed and homely: the kitchen has primrose walls and cheerfully painted blue chairs and window-frames, though the great grey stone fireplace is beautifully austere. A door leads out to a shingled terrace and garden for sunny breakfasts. Pastel and white bedrooms, with wooden floors and pretty fabrics, are quietly understated. Explore the area's delightful villages by foot or bicycle — it's flat, so even novices will manage.

Sleeps: 7.
Price: €678-€838 (£425-£525).
Bedrooms: 2 doubles; 1 twin; 1 single; 2 showers & wc.

Booking details:
Hugh & Crystal St John Mildmay
Tel: +44 (0)1453 542140

Map no: 11

Moreau, 17270 Cercoux

Understated elegance and homeliness are skilfully combined in this gorgeous 18th-century farmhouse. Plain yet luxurious, its mood of tranquillity and sophistication beguiles and soothes. It is decorated throughout with beautiful antiques and it's no surprise to learn that the helpful English owner Marian, who lives next door, is a professional antiques dealer. The house used to be a wealthy farm where *Pineau* was made, and features such as the chestnut beamed ceilings and stone fireplace have been superbly preserved. The spectacular kitchen — the old distillery — has a huge vaulted ceiling, a woodburning range, and dazzling white walls and floors which set off the fine display of navy and white china. Enjoy the dreamy views over the fields from the carpeted double bedroom, with a fabulous antique bed under huge beams. Buy basic supplies in nearby Cercoux, or shop at the twice-weekly market at pretty Coutras, 20 minutes' drive away. Nearby medieval Montguyon holds an annual folklore festival in July and August.

Sleeps: 4-7.
Price: €319-€621 (£200-£390).
Bedrooms: 2 doubles, 1 with extra single, bathroom & wc, 1 with wc; 1 double sofabed; shower & wc.

Booking details:
Marian Sanders
Tel: +33 (0)5 46 04 01 66
Fax: +33 (0)5 46 04 01 66
E-mail: marianatmoreau@hotmail.com

Le Masbeau, 23400 Saint Dizier Leyrenne

Roam the farm's 200 hectares on horseback, explore this sparsely populated area by bike or on foot — or just sit and ponder in the garden. Grain was once stored in the upper floor of the house, which dates from the 1780s. It's been skilfully converted into three carpeted bedrooms and a living room, all with sloping woodbeamed ceilings. Downstairs, where the farmworkers used to live, there's a dining room with a woodburner, exposed stone walls and simple furniture, a small functional kitchen and a lovely breakfast room with views of the horses in the fields. There's a patio and a little private garden, although you can share the Pélège family's much larger one. Nothing is too much trouble for your hosts Nicole and Jean-Pierre: he, a born enthusiast, farms cows; she is sunny natured and was once a nurse. You can buy fresh organic vegetables from the next-door farm which also runs an auberge. If you don't fancy riding, walking, or cycling, relax by the shared pool or watch the goings-on of a true working farm. Children will love it.

Sleeps: 6-12.
Price: €558-€901 (£350-£565).
Bedrooms: 1 double with shower room ensuite; 2 doubles, each with extra bunk bed, shower rooms ensuite; sofabed in living room.

Booking details:
Nicole & Jean-Pierre Pelege
Tel: +33 (0)5 55 64 40 11
E-mail: j-p.pelege@wanadoo.fr
Web: web.net-time.net/masbeau

Map no: 7

The Bakehouse, Le Prézat, 19380 Albussac

Anne and Jim chose to move from England to this region because it "looked lumpy" on the map and there weren't too many Brits. In the lush rolling hills of the Corrèze, this tiny cottage, once a bakehouse, is a perfect retreat for two. You'll want to join the Lardners' B&B guests for the odd four-course dinner — Anne's home-grown cooking is unmissable — but you have total privacy too, with your own section of garden (partially shaded by an ancient walnut tree) where you can sunbathe or barbecue. Furniture is basic with no frills and the house is mostly carpeted. The kitchen, with terracotta tiled floor and white formica worktops, was originally the bread oven. A dear little bedroom tucked under the pine-clad gabled roof has exposed stone walls and pastel-coloured bedcovers. Rouse yourself in the mornings with a brisk two-kilometre walk to buy fresh bread and croissants at the *boulangerie* in Albussac. There's golf and fishing nearby and the historic towns of Rocamadour and Collonges-la-Rouge are a short drive. Or just flop at Le Prézat.

Sleeps: 2.
Price: €260-€335.
Bedrooms: 1 twin; shower & wc.

Booking details:
Anne & Jim Lardner
Tel: +33 (0)5 55 28 62 36
Fax: +33 (0)5 55 28 62 36
E-mail: jlardner@libertysurf.fr

Map no: 12

Main House, Fleuret, 19500 Curemonte

The setting of this 17th-century farmhouse is breathtaking: there are magnificent views of rolling hills and woodland on all sides and the medieval hilltop village of Curemonte is just three kilometres away. Although close to the busy Dordogne river, Fleuret, once a hamlet of 12 families, stands in its own secret valley. It's been sensitively restored by Gilly and her architect/photographer husband Tim, whose photographs you'll see around the place. The young, easy-going owners live with their two children in another part of the house, but walls are thick and space is plentiful so they won't impinge. The welcoming kitchen/dining room has warm wood flooring, a woodburner in the ancient fireplace and a wonderful table for family feasts, and there's a sitting room with terracotta-washed walls, exposed stonework and sofas to lounge in. Apart from one double bedroom downstairs, bedrooms are on the attic floor with gabled ceilings and fabulous views. If you can tear yourselves away, there are castles, caves and canoeing.

Sleeps: 10.
Price: €1,101-€1,899 (£690-£1,190).
Bedrooms: 2 doubles with shower & wc; 1 twin; 1 triple; 1 single; bathroom & wc.

Booking details:
Tim & Gilly Mannakee
Tel: +33 (0)5 55 84 06 47
Fax: +33 (0)5 55 84 05 73
E-mail: info@fleuretholidays.com
Web: www.fleuretholidays.com

Map no: 12

The Cottage, Fleuret, 19500 Curemonte

You can still see the old bread oven in the kitchen, its brick surround charred by the ages. It was excavated by your delightful young British hosts, Tim and Gilly, who have restored this red sandstone farm cottage with imagination and sensitivity. Stonework and ancient roof beams have been carefully preserved and terracotta floors and pine cupboards added, while strings of garlic and cookery books show this to be a genuine family home. Bedrooms are cosy and carpeted, and the twin has a bedside table made from the bread oven chimney breast. French doors lead from the airy sitting/dining room to an outdoor dining and barbecue area where you can eat in privacy and soak up fabulous views of fields, woods and rolling hills and the 11th-century village of Curemonte. There's a huge pool, shared with the main house next door, and an amazing barn with a vast solid oak floor which you are free to use for what you like, from table tennis to dancing. You'll find it hard to drag children away. A perfect home for a small family in search of peace and space.

Sleeps: 4.
Price: €511-€941 (£320-£590).
Bedrooms: 1 double; 1 twin; bathroom & wc.

Booking details:
Tim & Gilly Mannakee
Tel: +33 (0)5 55 84 06 47
Fax: +33 (0)5 55 84 05 73
E-mail: info@fleuretholidays.com
Web: www.fleuretholidays.com

Map no: 12

Aquitaine

Photography by Michael Busselle.

Le Noyer, 24340 Saint Felix de Bourdeilles

The walnut tree which gave the farmhouse its name was blown down in a recent storm, but otherwise little seems to have changed for centuries in this unspoiled landscape. Sheep graze lazily in the seven acres of fields and woods surrounding the house, and life continues much as it always has in the pretty village of Saint Felix de Bourdeilles across the valley. Bridget and Pete, both teachers, live discreetly in a wing of the house during British school holidays. They've restored it with taste and skill. Wonderful warm beams, Shaker-style green-painted cupboards and a terracotta tile floor give a welcoming atmosphere to the kitchen/dining room, and it's prettily decorated with English china, country antiques and ceramic sink tiles. Enjoy the serene views out of the windows, or eat out on the terrace. Bedrooms have high vaulted ceilings with white painted beams, pine-boarded floors and small floor-level windows, while bathrooms are carpeted. Walking is good around here, or visit Brantôme with its famous weekly market. Ideal for families with young children.

Sleeps: 6.
Price: €479-€797 (£300-£500).
Bedrooms: 2 doubles, 1 with bathroom; 1 room with bunkbeds; bathroom.

Booking details:
Bridget & Pete Jones
Tel: +44 (0)1189 411737
E-mail: bridget@rcol.org.uk

Le Pigeonnier, La Geyrie, 24320 Verteillac

A pair of nesting barn owls has taken up residence in the tower of this fine 15th-century *pigeonnier*. You may spot short-toed eagles and roe deer in the surrounding fields and woods, too. You won't find luxury here — furnishings are basic and well-used — but you'll enjoy the simple rural life of a small farmstead; chickens, dogs and cats roam the courtyard, and Louise, the down-to-earth and dedicated English owner, raises goats organically (children may get a chance to watch them being milked and you can buy the milk). Louise lives with her husband and two teenage children in the old farmhouse, and there's one other rented house, too. Inside, the *pigeonnier* is pleasantly cool, with tiled floors, exposed beams and an old stone fireplace. Walk in the newly designated Limousin-Perigord National Park (one kilometre away), or enjoy the collection of rare orchids in the private Limodore reserve nearby. *No washing machine or dishwasher.*

Sleeps: 2 + 1-2 children.
Price: €175-€415 (£110-260).
Bedrooms: 1 double plus single bed; single bed downstairs in kitchen/diner; shower & wc.

Booking details:
Louise & Peter Dunn
Tel: +33 (0)5 53 91 15 15
Fax: +33 (0)5 53 90 37 19
E-mail: peter.dunn@wanadoo.fr
Web: perso.wanadoo.fr/gites.at.la.geyrie

Map no: 12

Bourdil Blanc, 24520 Saint Sauveur de Bergerac

All this could be yours: a fine 18th-century manor with a long, tree-lined avenue, views down to the lake and a 72m² swimming pool. When you're not lazing in the huge grounds or being sporty around tennis or croquet balls, retreat to the sitting room, with its comfortably lived-in sofas and superb bookcases flanking the fireplace. For more formal moments the magnificent dining room seats 14 on upholstered chairs and has William Morris-type fabric wall-coverings and curtains, a mirrored fireplace and polished floors. Upstairs, a wonderful long, light passage leads to the bedrooms which are more plainly dressed. The sunny kitchen and the bathrooms too are more functional than fabulous. The Wing is less grand than the main house but has an open fire, tiled floors, warm kilim rugs, some good antiques and a separate kitchen. Perfect for a mixed group, with space indoors and out to gather and disband, and stacks to do in the area. *Cooking and baby-sitting available. Security deposit of £400 payable when booking.*

Sleeps: 8-10; Wing 2-4; Pigeonnier 4.
Price: €2,175-€6,365 (£1,350-£3,950).
Bedrooms: 2 doubles, 1 twin, all en suite; 1 twin; 3 sofabeds; bath. Wing: 1 double; 2 sofabeds; bath & wc. Pigeonnier: 2 doubles, 1 twin, bath & wc.

Booking details:
Jane Hanslip
Tel: +44 (0)207 727 8014
Fax: +44 (0)207 221 6909
E-mail: jhanslip@aol.com
Web: www.dordognerental.com

La Martigne, 24520 Lamonzie-Montastruc

This glorious stone *chartreuse* could be nowhere else but France. Very French, it's a pleasing mix of simple and luxurious, unadorned and ornate. Splendidly isolated, with magnificent views of the Perigord Noir, the house has been beautifully restored by its French owners, who have lived here for generations. They occasionally use the pool, but otherwise the cascading terraced lawns, the private park and the pool are yours to enjoy. The house is furnished with dark antiques which contrast with the simple blue-green doors with old porcelain handles, the bare stone and the plain painted walls. The two living rooms have polished wooden floors, comfy sofas and elegant blue and white upholstered Regency chairs; next door there's a formal dining room with rich red wallpaper and attractive rugs. Bedrooms, huge and light, are furnished with antiques and open onto the south-facing terrace with lovely views. *Security deposit of £400 payable when booking.*

Sleeps: 8-9.
Price: €1,128-€2,578 (£700-1,600).
Bedrooms: 2 doubles, 1 with extra single bed; 2 twins; bathroom; shower; 2 wcs.

Booking details:
Jane Hanslip
Tel: +44 (0)207 727 8014
Fax: +44 (0)207 221 6909
E-mail: jhanslip@aol.com
Web: www.dordognerental.com

Map no: 12

La Treille Haute, 24250 Castelnaud-la-Chapelle

The setting smacks of a fairytale and five of the Perigord's most spectacular châteaux, clinging to the craggy cliffs of the River Dordogne, lie within three kilometres of your beautiful converted stone barn. You can even see the floodlit Château de Beynac, awesome and grand, from the comfort of your bed. By day, buy some local *foie gras* and picnic in the rich fields and wooded hills or stroll among the warm stone houses of La Roque-Gageac, often described as the most beautiful village in France. English owner Felicity — she has been a dancer, a singer, a member of the Navy, and is now a grandmother — lives in the house at right angles to the barn but three-foot-thick walls between the two buildings mean total privacy and you have your own large garden with staggering views. Furnishings are modest, although exposed stone walls and, in the bedroom, old oak beams, speak of the days when the building sheltered pilgrims of the Knights Templar. *Babies and children over four welcome. Babysitting available.*

Sleeps: 2-3 + 1 baby.
Price: €297-€457.
Bedrooms: 1 double with extra single bed and cot; shower & wc. Folding bed on request.

Booking details:
Felicity Martindale
Tel: +33 (0)5 53 29 95 65
Fax: +33 (0)5 53 29 95 65
E-mail: martindale@perigord.com

Lavande, 24250 Cénac-et-Saint-Julien

Brigitte and Christophe spotted this 18th-century farmhouse and 10-hectare estate while on holiday. It was love at first sight — a *coup de cœur* as Brigitte puts it — and five busy years on they run an enchanting B&B and have converted the stone stables into two self-catering cottages. Lavande, with its serene views over wooded hills, is the largest and, despite the proximity of the other buildings, is peaceful and private. The inside has been thoroughly restored — some might say too thoroughly — and despite the old beams and exposed walls, has a new feel. The living room has sumptuous black leather armchairs and sofa which provide a foil to the immaculately polished wooden floor. The *pièce de resistance*, however, is the beamed white and blue bedroom which looks like a piece of Delft china. Gourmets will make a beeline for the restaurant L'Esplanade in Domme, but if you prefer home-cooking join Brigitte, Christophe and their B&B guests for dinner in the farmhouse. And do buy Brigitte's delicious home-made pâtés for your picnic baguettes.

Sleeps: 6.
Price: €576-€1,050.
Bedrooms: Ground-floor double with shower & wc; 1 double with bathroom; 1 attic twin; wc.

Booking details:
Brigitte Demassogne
Tel: +33 (0)5 53 29 91 97
Fax: +33 (0)5 53 30 23 89
E-mail: contact@la-gueriniere-dordogne.com
Web: www.la-gueriniere-dordogne.com

Map no: 12

La Grange, La Font Trémolasse, 24510 Sainte-Alvère

Once you'd have heard the ruminating of cows in this house: as its name suggests, this was a barn and a cowshed, and the old chestnut cowstalls divide the kitchen and living room, the headholes forming perfect hatches. The cottage is the ground floor of a wing of a vast 19th-century Perigordine farmhouse, restored and lived in by hardworking British owners Victoria and Julius and their three children. He's a landscape gardener and will supply herbs if you need them; she used to cook professionally and will lay on dinner using their own produce if you book. There's a sunny modern kitchen with hardwood work surfaces and terracotta tiled floor, in contrast to the rather old fashioned 'genteel' living/dining room. The bedroom, wooden-floored with cheerful red curtains, has tranquil views of the garden and fields of the 45-acre estate. Eat outside on your private south-facing terrace, swim, fish or sail (dinghy provided) in the lake, or visit the many prehistoric caves in the area. Sainte-Alvère, the nearest village, is famous for its truffles.

Sleeps: 2.
Price: €311-€399 (£195-£250).
Bedrooms: 1 twin/double; bathroom
& wc.

Booking details:
Victoria White
Tel: +33 (0)5 53 23 94 33
Fax: +33 (0)5 53 23 94 87
E-mail: vjwhite@club-internet.fr

Les Bigayres, 24520 Liorac-sur-Louyre

Enjoy the bedrooms in this elegant converted *pigeonnier*: one has old gnarled beams which seem to grow like trees through the tall pointed ceiling, another has an amazing *Princess and the Pea* bed with the highest mattress you have ever seen. And teenagers will love the third — a bunk bedroom with its own poolside entrance. In 33 acres of grounds belonging to a lovely 17th-century manor house, with its own private drive and terrace, this beautifully furnished cottage is a real find. You share the pool with the French lawyer owners, but they are rarely there so you are most likely to have it to yourself. The kitchen/living/dining room — pure, light and roomy — is so stunning you'll find it hard to pull yourself away. The sitting area has white or exposed stone walls, grey-green beams supported by unusual stone columns, and generous, floor-to-ceiling, tomato-red and green curtains. Wallow in the luxurious sofas by the stone fireplace, or stroll out of the French doors to the lawn with its long wooded views. *£200 security deposit payable when booking.*

Sleeps: 6-8.
Price: €725-€1,537 (£450-£950).
Bedrooms: 2 doubles, 1 downstairs; 1 twin (bunks) – outside entry; 1 double sofabed; bathroom & wc.

Booking details:
Jane Hanslip
Tel: +44 (0)207 727 8014
Fax: +44 (0)207 221 6909
E-mail: jhanslip@aol.com
Web: www.dordognerental.com

Map no: 12

La Boétie, Domaine de la Plumardie, 24510 Sainte-Alvère

It was here in the wooded Vézère valley that the first skeletons of Cro-Magnon people, the first *Homo Sapiens*, were unearthed in the mid-19th century, and you'll find an overwhelming choice of prehistoric cave paintings to visit during your stay at this imposing 17th-century farmstead. Enthusiastic and effusive owners Henriette and Dieter have sympathetically converted the lovely stone buildings that embrace a central courtyard and turned them into holiday cottages, of which La Boétie — named after the local writer — is the smallest. The buildings have been skilfully designed to ensure maximum privacy and the only place you're likely to encounter your neighbours is around the pool. The south-facing compact kitchen/living room, with tiled floor and cream walls, has fine views over the wooded valley on one side, and on the other, over a gravelled terrace bordered with lavender and rosemary where you can eat out. Furnishings are modern, mostly pine, although old beams have been kept in the carpeted bedroom. Excellent value.

Sleeps: 3-4.
Price: €206-€336.
Bedrooms: 1 triple (3 single beds);
sofabed in living room; shower & wc.

Booking details:
Henriette & Dieter Muller
Tel: +33 (0)5 53 03 34 64
Fax: +33 (0)5 53 03 34 64
E-mail: laplumardie@free.fr

Map no: 12

Le Branchat, 24170 Sagelat

Richard is half-Spanish, used to be a hotelier and now paints; Isabelle's French, a mum and a part-time air hostess; both are enthusiasts, and will ensure your stay here is one you won't forget. The highlight is the garden — seven hectares of it — which combines fruit and nut orchards with forests, fields grazed by the family donkey, pony, chickens and ducks, and a deliciously huge (fenced, shared) swimming pool. Share your adventures over dinner with the family and their B&B guests: the Ginioux make their own *confits* and pâtés which are unmissable. The cottage had been energetically modernised by its previous owners, but the Ginioux have made the most of the clean modern lines and pure white walls, decorating with unfussy fabrics and solid, high-quality woods. The kitchen/dining room has beautiful polished wooden floors and furniture handmade by a family friend. Bedrooms under the gables are in sunny yellows and creams. Be sure to visit the beautiful hilltop village of Belvès and its old pillared market.

Sleeps: 4-5.
Price: €305-€610.
Bedrooms: 1 double; 1 double with extra single bed; shower & wc.

Booking details:
Richard & Isabelle Ginioux
Tel: +33 (0)5 53 28 98 80
Fax: +33 (0)5 53 28 90 82
E-mail: le.branchat@wanadoo.fr
Web: www.perigord.com/belves/lebranchat

Map no: 12

Le Sage, 24500 Eymet

When Caroline and her artist husband bought this ancient *pigeonnier* they found just four limestone walls and a mulberry tree in a forest of weeds. Thirty years on, the tree still stands, the tower and wing next door have gained a roof and stylish furnishings, and the garden's been tamed into an inspirational glow of colour. Gardening is Caroline's passion, and she'll bring you fresh vegetables and fruit when there's a surplus; enjoy cherries and tomatoes in summer, and delicious butternut squash in autumn. Dress them with home-grown herbs, or, if you want a rest, Caroline, who lives across the garden, will cook you dinner. Bright and pleasant rooms have simple, comfortable furnishings and white or exposed stone walls, many of them hung with paintings by Caroline's husband. The attractive kitchen in the base of the tower has doors leading to a private vine-covered terrace from where you can enjoy views over the valley of the River Dropt. Caroline, easy-going and down-to-earth, will advise on Romanesque churches, castles and canoeing.

Sleeps: 4.
Price: €239-€447 (£150-£280).
Bedrooms: 1 twin; 1 double; shower & wc.

Booking details:
Caroline Portway
Tel: +33 (0)5 53 24 50 66
Fax: +33 (0)5 53 24 50 66
E-mail: caroline@stain.org
Web: www.stain.org/sage

Map no: 12

Le Moulin de Sorreau, 24230 Montcaret

Water, water everywhere. Watch it tumbling over rocks in the mill stream which encircles the house, cool your toes in it, allow its soft sound to soothe you to sleep. Carp swim in the mill pool, fed by cascading waterfalls, and lush vegetation creates dancing dappled shade on the big lawns and paddock. This ancient stone mill has been sensitively restored by Bryan, a composer, and John, a watercolour painter, who moved here in search of space and inspiration. They live in the building next door; kindred artistic spirits will enjoy their company. The room where the old mill machinery still stands is a music studio, with a piano. The living/dining room, with white walls and a working fireplace, feels homely rather than sophisticated, and there's an old-fashioned but adequate kitchen. Bedrooms, simple and elegant, have polished wood floors, old country furniture, and, naturally, water views. In summer, witness the re-enactment of the Hundred Years' War at Castillion-la-Bataille. *Not suitable for small children.*

Sleeps: 5.
Price: €319-€558 (£200-£350).
Bedrooms: 2 doubles; 1 single; bathroom & wc; wc.

Booking details:
John Newberry & Bryan Kelly
Tel: +33 (0)5 53 27 37 14
Fax: +33 (0)5 53 27 37 14

Map no: 12

Le Petit Tilleul, 24250 Domme

The Dordogne river is only 150 metres from the door and busy Domme is just up the hill, but here is total peace. This compact stone cottage — built around 1650 as a hay barn, later converted into the baker's house — has the best of both worlds. Friendly owners Mary and Alan live in another farm building (where they do B&B) along the lane: you can book painting lessons with Mary, once an art teacher. Alan taught design and woodwork, and you'll see his handiwork in their simple but successful conversion. Downstairs, old beams and stone walls are all intact and there's a woodburner in the beautiful stone fireplace in the living room. The well-lit kitchen has white formica worktops and French windows onto the terrace and garden, perfect for eating out. Bedrooms are simple, with wooden shutters and open hanging space. The double has views of Domme and fields; the twin is furnished in pine. Your problem will be to decide what to do first: there's swimming in the Dordogne, the picturesque GR64A footpath runs past the door, and Domme and medieval Sarlat are both a delight.

Sleeps: 4.
Price: €350-€600.
Bedrooms: 1 double; 1 twin; shower & wc.

Booking details:
Alan & Mary Johnson
Tel: +33 (0)5 53 29 39 96
Fax: +33 (0)5 53 29 39 96
E-mail: montillou@hotmail.com

Map no: 12   85

La Gouraude, 33580 Rimons

Your only neighbours are the owls in the woods which surround this 300-year old farmhouse and its gardens; the nearest humans live a mile away. Stroll down the stone path which meanders across the lawns to the pool, or relax among the wisteria and geraniums on the tiled veranda. You even have your own stream, reached through a tunnel in the woods; children will love the games room in the barn opposite and the Wendy house. Slightly more modest and mellow than Christopher and Louise's other houses, La Gourade has been decorated to the same high standard, with antiques, gay rugs, and high-quality fabrics. Original features like the old stone basin built into the sitting room wall and the great oak beams have been carefully kept. Bedrooms, in the old granary, have stunning antique beds and white walls hung with pretty china plates and paintings. Visit the Cathar stronghold of Montségur and its evocative château, from where you can take the dramatic four-hour walk to the Têt valley over the Montagne de la Frau.

Sleeps: 12.
Price: €1,427-€3,069 (£895-£1,925); up to 5 people, €1,036-€1,873 (£650-£1,175).
Bedrooms: 4 twins; 2 doubles; bathroom & wc; 2 showers & wc.

Booking details:
Christopher & Louise Taylor
Tel: +33 (0)5 53 20 88 03
Fax: +33 (0)5 53 83 61 79
E-mail: taylor.christophe@wanadoo.fr

Map no: 12

Moulin du Cros, 33190 Hure

Mill streams and ancient bridges, a circular stone tower and even your very own island: this is a really magical place to keep cool on summer days. The mill, parts of which date from the 14th century, has been in the owner's family for several generations, and each has restored another section. There's still work for future generations: the vaulted middle part, which connects the two sides of the house, is virtually untouched and still contains the ancient millstones and stone floor. You'll come here for the dreamy river views, wild flowers and wonderful natural surroundings rather than for sophisticated décor. The large dining/living room has exposed stone walls, yellow Provençal curtains and cushions and a relaxed feel. There's a small basic kitchen at one end, with stairs leading up to two bedrooms above. Those who really want to escape can retreat to the double bedroom in the watch tower which has its own entrance. Relax on the many grassed terraces, flop into the pool, or fish for eel or trout in the river. *Tower rented alone in low season.*

Sleeps: 10-12.
Price: €2,300-€2,750.
Bedrooms: 4 doubles, 1 with wc, 1 with bathroom & wc, 1 with shower & wc; 1 twin; bathroom & wc.

Booking details:
Fabienne Guipouy-Lafargue
Tel: +33 (0)5 56 61 21 85 (eve)
Fax: +33 (0)5 53 20 11 47
E-mail: Fguipouy@aol.com

L'Heritier, Parranquet, 47210 Villeréal

You'll not want to leave this tranquil farmstead in the rolling Quercian countryside. Read, eat or snooze in the blissfully private, shaded courtyard in front of the house, enclosed on both sides by wonderful stone barns; or cool off in the pool with views of fields and an ancient *pigeonnier* (also rented). Bird watchers and nature lovers will love it: look out for hoopoes and bee orchids. Homely, well-loved and informal in feel, the house is perfect for one or two families with children. On cool evenings enjoy dinner around the refectory table in the oak-beamed living room warmed by the woodburning stove. Attractive English and French country furniture, chestnut floors, well-used rugs and a fireside settle create a cosy atmosphere. Bedrooms, in two separate sets, are on the basic side, with rather elderly mattresses giving the air of a provincial country hotel. But some will find nostalgia in the naively floral wallpapers, and the master bedroom has a lovely antique bed and polished wood floor.

Sleeps: 9.
Price: €798-€1,516 (£500-£950).
Bedrooms: 2 doubles, 1 connected to twin; 1 triple (3 singles); bathroom & wc.

Booking details:
Jane Quincey
Tel: +44 (0)1503 240599
Fax: +44 (0)1503 240599
E-mail: jquincey@mistral.co.uk
Web: www.farmhouseinfrance.com

Map no: 12

Château de Rodié, 47370 Courbiac de Tournon

Meditate in the candlelit tower, amble through the vast banqueting hall, and take a dip in the pool discreetly hidden behind the south façade of this fairytale château. The story of how Pippa, her husband Paul and their two daughters and dog have breathed new life into these old, old stones is inspiring: Paul had a serious car accident, they bought the ruined 13th-century hill-top château and its 135 acres of grounds, and, stone by stone, began the mammoth task of restoration. Passionately committed to preserving its history, they retrieved all the original materials, from *pisé* floors in the tower to ancient stone fireplaces and ceiling beams. When they're not educating their bi-lingual girls, Paul and Pippa farm sheep organically and run a B&B. Pippa also finds the time to cook delicious dinners, using their own produce — book in advance. Reached from the arched courtyard, the apartment has its own private terrace off the kitchen/living room: eat outside and savour the beauty of this magical place.

Sleeps: 7-9.
Price: €572-€1,145.
Bedrooms: 2 doubles, 1 with bathroom & wc, 1 with extra single; 1 twin with bathroom & wc; 2 extra singles on request.

Booking details:
Paul & Pippa Hecquet
Tel: +33 (0)5 53 40 89 24
Fax: +33 (0)5 53 40 89 25
E-mail: chateau.rodie@wanadoo.fr

Map no: 12

Villas, 47210 Villeréal

Very traditional, very French, this solid 18th-century Perigordian stone farmhouse gives a glimpse of old, rural France. A week here, and you'll be steeped in it. Rooms are big, sensitively restored, and decorated with beautiful well-loved antiques. Look out for the cute antique blue and white wash basin with brass taps in the entrance hall, and for the lights in the dining room which hang, like bells, from an ancient ox-yoke. There's a vast stone fireplace in here, and French windows which lead out to the terrace (where you can eat out) and big peaceful lawns. Carpeted bedrooms have *lits bâteaux* which children will enjoy, and dark antiques which contrast with the colourful bedcovers. This place is ideal for two families holidaying together, and you'll have total privacy as the owners move to Brittany for the summer. Enjoy a late night dip in the floodlit pool and by day visit the 13th-century *bastides* of Villeréal with its lovely oak-beamed *halles* in the central square, and Montflanquin. *June-September lets only.*

Sleeps: 8.
Price: €1,220- €1,830.
Bedrooms: 2 doubles with shower;
1 four-bed room with bathroom; 2 wcs.

Booking details:
Henri & Monique Lefebre
Tel: +33 (0)5 53 36 60 18

Map no: 12

Chalet des Rigals, 47330 Castillonnès

The sensational cherry-tree-lined drive to the house says it all: Patricia and David's passion is trees and they've planted 400 new ones since they moved here five years ago. They've forged trails through their woods where, if you're lucky, you can find 17 types of wild orchid. The Babers also love gardening and will probably offer you fresh vegetables or eggs from their Bantams. The 150-year-old house once accommodated the guardian of the manor house, a short stroll away, where your hosts and their B&B guests live. Inside, it's homely and unaffected, with check curtains, terracotta floors, and a round table and wheel-back chairs in the kitchen/dining room. On cool evenings you can sit on friendly old-fashioned sofas and chairs in front of the woodburner in the sitting room. Bedrooms are frilly and light, with padded bedheads and matching quilt-covers and lamps. Downstairs there is a twin leading to a double, and upstairs there is a huge dormitory under the eaves, great for children. *Tennis court available.*

Sleeps: 6-8.
Price: €915-€1,830.
Bedrooms: 1 double with ensuite shower room; 1 twin; 1 attic room with 4 singles; bathroom; wc.

Booking details:
David & Patricia Baber
Tel: +33 (0)5 53 41 24 21
Fax: +33 (0)5 53 41 24 79
E-mail: babersrig@aol.com
Web: www.ecu.co.uk/rigals

Le Pas de l'Ane, 47330 Lalandusse

Simplicity and taste characterise this immaculately converted *pigeonnier* and barn. Beams and antiques contrast with whitewashed or exposed stone walls and there's a light airy feel throughout. The setting is hard to fault too, with long lazy views over grazed fields, a small lawn, and a large swimming pool to the side. There's little apart from the odd tractor to disturb you here, and although Lydia and her potter husband, Christian, live 50 metres away they'll not disturb your privacy. Our favourite room is the double bedroom at the top of the house which has a beautiful exposed gable ceiling, a comfortable bed with luxurious white bedcovers, and antique country furniture. The kitchen/dining room has a welcoming table with ladder-back chairs, a terracotta floor and solid wood kitchen cupboards. Rustle up the odd *ratatouille* in the top-quality stainless steel pans; eat outside if you wish. On the border of the Dordogne and the Lot-et-Garonne there are plenty of medieval châteaux and bastide towns to visit.

Sleeps: 7.
Price: €690-€1,100.
Bedrooms: 2 doubles; 1 room with bunkbeds; 1 single & cot; 2 wcs; bathroom on ground floor.

Booking details:
Lydia Freymuth
Tel: +33 (0)5 53 36 96 08
Fax: +33 (0)5 53 36 97 06

Map no: 12

Marcou, 47150 Monflanquin

You're in *bastide* country here, and of all the hillfort villages, 13th-century Monflanquin is perhaps the most perfectly preserved. Walk there in just 20 minutes, or gaze upon it, perched proud above the surrounding fields, from the tranquillity of your terrace. The house is part of a 17th-century stone farmstead, owned by friendly Belgian hosts, Bernard, Nathalie and their four children, who live across the courtyard. The house can be rented as a whole, or as two separate cottages, each sleeping eight. Downstairs rooms are large and light with exposed stone or rendered walls, old beams and easy-to-clean terracotta tiled floors. The old bread oven and a collection of old wirelesses add interest, and you'll see Nathalie's artistic touch (she's an interior designer) in the decorative brickwork. Bedrooms are mostly small and basic, with new pine furniture and open hanging space. Relax by the pool, or on cooler days, pay to use the de Woelmont's state-of-the-art jacuzzi. Ideal for families holidaying together.

Sleeps: 16 + 2 babies.
Price: €800-€2,500.
Bedrooms: 4 doubles, 3 with bath/shower & wc, 1 with extra bunkbeds; 2 rooms with bunkbeds, 1 with 3 extra beds; shower; 2 wcs.

Booking details:
Bernard de Woelmont
Tel: +33 (0)5 53 36 33 27
Fax: +33 (0)5 53 36 33 27
E-mail: gitemarcou@libertysurf.fr
Web: www.perso.wanadoo.fr/bernard.de-woelmont/

Map no: 12

As Bernis, 47290 Beaugas

You're in deep prune country — and plums used to be dried in the three magnificent brick-clad ovens in the living room wall. This 18th-century stone building was once a farmhouse, and it's taken Pierre and Annick 18 dedicated years to convert it into the gorgeous home it now is. They've skilfully teased out the building's original character by recycling old materials wherever possible: old wood has been reused to make bannisters and ancient stones have been turned into steps or ledges. You even have your own bar, picked up by Pierre from an antique dealer, where you can serve yourself a tipple and sip it at a bistro-style metal table. The huge sitting/dining room has lovely solid antique furniture, a stone fireplace, and a stunning original quarry tile and wooden board floor. Bedrooms are large and simple, with generous windows and views of the wide lawn and woods outside. A garden spring feeds two small ponds and there's a peaceful terrace for *al fresco* dining. Buy your prunes in Villeneuve-sur-Lot, and visit Cancon and Monflanquin. *Table tennis & volley ball court available.*

Sleeps: 8-12.
Price: €1,100-€2,135.
Bedrooms: 4 doubles, 1 with shower & wc; 1 room with 4 singles & baby bed; shower; bathroom; 2 wcs.

Booking details:
Pierre & Annick Durin
Tel: +33 (0)5 53 01 76 83
E-mail: asbernis@libertysurf.fr
Web: perso.libertysurf.fr/as_bernis

Map no: 12

Manoir Coutenson, 47250 Grezet-Cavagnan

The electronically controlled gates and the sweeping gravel drive signal grandness and luxury and this 17-century manor house doesn't disappoint: a large heated pool in a floodlit walled garden, gorgeous antique furniture, and a cellar stocked with 100 bottles of wine. As if that weren't enough, a stone tower, snug for two, and a full-time gardener, are thrown in, too. This and the neighbouring farmhouse were discovered four years ago by Louise, who's French, and her English husband, Christopher, who ran an architectural salvage business. China plates on the walls and artfully arranged pots of dried flowers make it feel like home. Downstairs rooms mostly have terracotta tiled floors and lovely twisted oak beamed ceilings. Upstairs bedrooms are reached by two separate staircases leading to landings so comfortable you'll want to go no further: one has an oak polished floor and an antique desk and chair. Eat under the veranda by the pool and roam the four acres of gardens.

Sleeps: 16.
Price: €2,390-€4,261 (£1,500-£2,675); 7 people €1,585-€2,390 (£995-£1,500).
Bedrooms: 6 doubles; 2 twins; all en suite except 1; bathroom & wc.

Booking details:
Christopher & Louise Taylor
Tel: +33 (0)5 53 20 88 03
Fax: +33 (0)5 53 83 61 79
E-mail: taylor.christophe@wanadoo.fr

Manoir Desiderata, 47250 Grezet-Cavagnan

Sip a gin and tonic by the floodlit pool as you watch the sun set over the distant hills and woods; Desiderata, spotless and newly restored, gently demands that you unwind. No effort has been spared by Louise and Christopher in adapting its 300-year-old stones to contemporary tastes and needs; if you enjoy oak beams and period furniture, you'll love it. The layout is unusual, with most rooms leading off a vast terracotta-floored sitting room. A balustraded walkway runs along its length leading to four mezzanine-level bedrooms; three bedrooms lead off it downstairs. Enjoy the views of woods and the 12th-century local church from the large tower bedroom, with sand-coloured exposed stone walls and pretty floral bedcovers. Visit the *bastide* town of Casteljaloux, on the edge of the pine forest of Les Landes, with its old timber-framed houses with projecting storeys. There's good walking, too. Ideal for two families holidaying together, and the Taylors will go out of their way to make sure you have everything you want.

Sleeps: 14.
Price: €2,390-€3,744 (£1,500-£2,350); up to 5 people, €1,585-€2,390 (£995-£1,500).
Bedrooms: 4 doubles; 3 twins; all have own shower & wc.

Booking details:
Christopher & Louise Taylor
Tel: +33 (0)5 53 20 88 03
Fax: +33 (0)5 53 83 61 79
E-mail: taylor.christophe@wanadoo.fr

Map no: 12

La Gare de Sos, 47170 Sainte-Maure-de-Peyriac

Once your wake-up call would have been the hoot of the 06h27 from Sos to Nérac, and the now silent platforms would have bustled with chatting passengers. This railway station, which finally ground to a halt in 1970, has been stunningly converted by its English owner David, who gave up a City of London career for life at the end of the line. He lives in the house when it's not rented out, and moves into the nearby village when it is. The former waiting-room and parcels office are now the living/dining room, and turn-of-the-century advertising posters, a 1924 timetable, and some of the original clocks adorn its walls. The old wooden benches on which passengers waited have been exchanged for comfy sofas, and beautiful terracotta tiles have replaced the wooden floorboards. The ticket office is now a superb kitchen and pantry; the original oak staircase leads up to the bedrooms in the former station master's apartment. There's a fabulous attic too, with four beds — and a model railway, of course, which children will love. Unmissable.

Sleeps: 10.
Price: £385-£1,450.
Bedrooms: 2 doubles; 1 twin;
4-bedded room; shower & wc;
bathroom & wc.

Booking details:
David Heath
Tel: +33 (0)5 53 97 09 93
Fax: +33 (0)5 53 97 09 93
E-mail: adavidheath@aol.com
Web: www.garedesos.com

Résidence Lilinita, Avenue Beaurivage, 64200 Biarritz

Watch the rolling waves of the Atlantic from every window. Perched on the cliffs above Biarritz's Côte des Basques surfing beach this luxury turret apartment, built by a Polish countess in 1905, has truly staggering views. If you ever tire of watching the surfers, gaze at the distant peaks of the Spanish Pyrenees along the coast to the south. You're well placed to test the delights of this resort, once fashionable among Victorian ladies for its winter warmth. Boutiques and restaurants are a five-minute walk, as is the Casino Municipal, restored to its 1930s grandeur. Don't be deceived by the apartment's turn-of-the-century exterior: inside it's impeccably modern. There's a state-of-the-art kitchen and a large dining/living room with spotless polished floors, and a futuristic central staircase that leads to two bedrooms with pristine white bedcovers and lovely antiques. Choose between the two south-facing balconies to eat, and watch the sun set over the sea. *No children under 15. Rates for two, or for longer stays, on request.*

Sleeps: 4.
Price: €820-€1,640.
Bedrooms: 2 doubles/twins, 1 with bathroom & wc, 1 with shower & wc.

Booking details:
Sue & Bill Barr
Tel: +33 (0)5 59 34 34 14
Fax: +33 (0)5 59 34 35 44
E-mail: barr.bill@online.fr
Web: www.summerflat.com

Map no: 16

La Maison en Tôle Ondulée

In spite of coruscating criticism of our choice we have decided in favour of this little house. It is every bit as authentic for its period as the Festival Hall in London, the Hoover building in west London, the Empire State in New York, the Taj Mahal in India. The corrugated materials were the miracle of their day – light, cheap and strong, available to the poor all over the world. The industrial colouring and minimalist style are back in fashion in an age of 'hip' hotels. In this example there is an unusual juxtaposition of vertical and horizontal sheets, suggesting a committed amateur construction and a certain urgency. Indeed, it might be described as charmingly lackadaisical, even ramshackle. Just off the main path and thus close to the scurrying of local traffic, it is nevertheless deep in a vast organic woodland garden. In winter the dark interior cleverly mirrors the dark mystery of the woods. It is a great place to stay on a hot summer night when one wants to be alone – for who would accompany you?

Sleeps: Up to a few fearless friends.
Price: Under a tenner for full, permanent ownership.
Bedrooms: Iron 'dividers' allow flexible personal space-creation.

Booking details:
Some bloke round the corner
Tel: Wouldn't tell us his number
Fax: We've tried and failed
E-mail: nobody@home.here
Web: www.shacksharing.fr

Map no: 16

Midi – Pyrénées

Photography by Michael Busselle.

Monteillet-Sanvensa, 12200 Villefranche-de-Rouergue

Lounge in a hammock in the garden and luxuriate in the views of fields and the hamlet of Sanvensa; walk across the Rouergue hills to the medieval towns of Bruniquel, Cordes and Gaillac; or explore the nearby *bastide* town of Villefranche-de-Rouergue. The solid stone farmhouse provides a good centre from which to explore this rugged and fascinating *département*. The interior is basic but comfortable, furniture and colours rustic and old-fashioned. There's a large open-plan living room with Seventies-style chairs and brick fireplace, from which a section can be curtained off to make an extra bedroom. Upstairs is a large white bedroom under the gables, and a pretty smaller one with blue carpets. Relaxed and knowledgeable owners Pierre and Monique run a B&B next door; Pierre, half French, half American, used to run a restaurant so be sure to join him and his guests for dinner in the courtyard one evening. Pierre will put you in touch with local farmers to buy fresh produce and pick up bread for you in the mornings if you ask. Great value.

Sleeps: 6.
Price: €300-€505.
Bedrooms: 1 double; 1 double with extra single bed; sofabed & single downstairs; bathroom; wc.

Booking details:
Monique & Pierre Bateson
Tel: +33 (0)5 65 29 81 01
Fax: +33 (0)5 65 65 89 52
E-mail: pbc.@wanadoo.fr

Map no: 13

100

Maison La Grande Combe, 12480 Saint Izaire

"I'll guarantee you'll come away from here feeling fantastic about life. It's a paradise," wrote our inspector. This magnificent 17th-century stone farmhouse is different from most entries in this book in that you are part of a community, energetically and enthusiastically run by serene Dutch owners Nelleke, a psychologist, and her partner Hans. By day you have the choice of joining group sessions on themes like relaxation, walking the rugged Aveyron hills and wooded valleys, or just roaming the lovely grounds. In the evenings you can cook in your snug apartment, or join the B&B guests for a wholesome dinner in the main part of the house. Hans grows organic vegetables and fruit (some of which he bottles) and makes scrumptious bread; Nelleke is a splendid creator of jams. There are two studios here, each with its own entrance and patio, and *de rigueur* old wooden beams. Furniture is new and simple. Swim in the Tarn, walk from the house. Or just be.

Sleeps: Each studio: 2.
Price: Each studio: €255–€318.
Bedrooms: Each studio: 1 double sofabed with shower & wc.

Booking details:
Hans & Nelleke Versteegen
Tel: +33 (0)5 65 99 45 01
Fax: +33 (0)5 65 99 48 41
E-mail: grande.combe@wanadoo.fr
Web: www.la-grande-combe.nl

Map no: 13

Le Moulin, 12200 Villefranche-de-Rouergue

Gaze into the tranquil waters of the ancient mill pond and feel the stresses of modern life dissolve. Surrounded by 40 acres of woodland and orchid-dotted meadows, all you'll hear from this fabulous 18th-century mill are the birds — listen for woodpeckers — and the rustling of trees. Sit on one of the terraces — choose sun or shade — to drink in the deep peace of this lovely place; or, if you feel more energetic, take out a rowing boat onto the millpond or explore this ruggedly beautiful region on foot or canoe. Inside, the English owners have preserved many of the mill's original features, from old beams in the living/dining room to the original *évier* (stone sink) in the kitchen. On autumn evenings, feast by the immense stone *cantou* (fireplace). From the four-poster upstairs, with its cream and rose floral canopy, listen to the tumbling millstream. Shop in Villefranche-de-Rouergue, clustered around a pretty 13th-century arcaded market square (market day is Thursday). *Not suitable for young children.*

Sleeps: 6-7.
Price: €677-€1,585 (£425-£995).
Bedrooms: 2 twins, 1 downstairs;
1 double with bathroom & wc; spare
bed on landing; shower; wc.

Booking details:
Edward & Sybil Roskill
Tel: +44 (0)207 703 4736
Fax: +44 (0)207 701 6158
E-mail: roskillesw@aol.com
Web: www.la-belle-france.com

Map no: 13

La Mothe, 12260 Salles Courbatiers

Walkers, wine-buffs and wildlife lovers will adore this little-discovered corner of *La France Profonde*, as the Aveyron is known. The road to the hamlet of La Mothe, in which the 200-year-old farmhouse stands, goes blissfully nowhere, and from the house you can stride out into rolling hills and woods. Inside the tone is solid, ancient and authentic: no fuss or clutter here. The Clarks, who live here for part of the year, have renovated the house with refreshing simplicity, showing off original stone walls, oak beams and fabulous original doors to lovely effect. There's a handsome vaulted kitchen with a large pine table and chairs, and you'll find food cupboards stocked with the basics for your stay (just replace what you use). Enjoy the views from the first-floor sitting room with its stone fireplace, superb Louis XIII *armoires*, and delicious cream and apricot soft furnishings. Bedrooms have a mix of pine and antique furniture, and there's a huge sunny yellow attic room which children will love. Savour the wines from Cahors, Gaillac and Marcillac.

Sleeps: 10-12.
Price: €766-€2,234 (£480-£1,400).
Bedrooms: 2 doubles with bath or shower & wc; 1 twin with shower & wc; 4-bed attic room with shower & wc.

Booking details:
Rosemary & Gordon Clark
Tel: +44 (0)1296 747045
Fax: +44 (0)870 0561224
E-mail: frenchhouses2@cs.com

Map no: 12

Château de la Garinie, 12220 Lugan

Rapunzel may be missing but the turrets, towers and tapestries are here. There'll be nothing to stop you letting your hair down in this imposing 14th-century château, for it's blissfully peaceful in this remote part of the Aveyron. The château's been beautifully restored and furnished by its delightful ex-hotelier owners, Don and Ian, who live in the old stable block. Climb the stone staircase which spirals its way up one of the towers into the château and you know you're in for something special: all is grand, sumptuous and very, very old. You'll find fabulous antiques, sparkling chandeliers and original creaking floorboards. In the evening, dress for a candelit dinner in the formal dining room watched by ancient family portraits. Retire to a canopied bed with luxurious linen, or soak in a bath buried in a tower. Explore the rugged, thickly wooded valleys of the Aveyron on foot or on horseback, or visit the hilltop villages of Cordes and Najac with their half-timbered stone-tiled houses. *Available June to September only.*

Sleeps: 10 + 1 baby.
Price: €1,840-€2,880.
Bedrooms: 2 canopied doubles with shower/bathroom & wc; 1 double; 2 twins; shower & wc.

Booking details:
Colin Bath
Tel: +44 (0)1572 724596 (day)
+44 (0)1572 722571 (eve)
Fax: +44 (0)1572 724596
E-mail: barbarabath@supanet.com

Map no: 12

Montarsés de Tayrac, 12440 La Salvetat Peyralés

It's easy to understand why the Riebens decided to up sticks from Picardy and move to this huge 19th-century farmhouse and converted barn, perched proudly on the top of a hill. Jacques indulges his passion for pure-bred horses (you'll see them grazing from your bedroom window), Jo runs B&B (for up to 10 guests), and the sun shines. Roam the estate's 30 hectares of fields and woods, fish in the private lake, and, if you can prove your equine competence (and insurance) Jacques will allow you to ride. Rooms are big and old-fashioned, furnished with a mix of antique and modern brought from Picardy. There's a large if sombre living/dining room downstairs, with great beams, and a compact kitchen area one end. Bedrooms are light and have stripped wooden floors, cream walls and open hanging space. Explore the *bastide* towns with their perfectly preserved arcaded market squares, including Villefranche-de-Rouergue and Najac. *House can be let for 10, 6 or 4. Prices on request. Winter lets available.*

Sleeps: 10 (or 6 + 4).
Price: €686-€838 (for 10).
Bedrooms: 2 twins; 3 doubles, 1 with shower & wc; bathroom & wc; shower & wc.

Booking details:
Jo & Jacques Rieben
Tel: +33 (0)5 65 81 46 10
Fax: +33 (0)5 65 81 46 10

Map no: 13

Maison Roxy, 32320 Peyrusse Grande

A rambling stone house that feels like a home, not a holiday let. Full of character, it's clearly been lived in and loved by its English owners. At the end of the village, its five-foot-thick centre wall was part of the fortifications in the 12th century. More recently the second sitting room served as the village cinema, which tells you the size of some of the rooms. Downstairs has a solid feel with hefty wooden beams and mostly antique furniture. The living room has comfy sofas, plenty of books and doors to the pool and garden. There's a beautiful stone fireplace in the dining room, and suspended pans and hand-crafted wooden cabinets give the kitchen an informal friendly feel. Bedrooms — once you've found them, they're all on different levels — have what the owners call "antique or interesting" furniture. Ancient brass bedsteads combine with brightly painted 1930s furniture, while children's rooms are furnished more functionally. You can borrow bikes to go off exploring, or play tennis and *pétanque* on the courts along the street.

Sleeps: 11 + 1 baby.
Price: €925-€1,994 (£580-£1,250).
Bedrooms: 1 twin on mezzanine;
3 doubles; 1 triple (3 singles) & cot;
2 showers; 2 wcs.

Booking details:
Alison Jones
Tel: +44 (0)1435 830395
E-mail: robin_jones@talk21.com

Petit Setzères, Setzères, 32230 Marciac

The house is the converted stables of a fine manor set on the soft slopes of this unspoilt part of rural France. Petit Setzères has a big, well-furnished ground-floor living area where you can snuggle down in front of a log fire with a book from those provided. Carry your lunch out into the lush garden and onto the terrace under a high old barn roof and marvel at the Pyrenees which look back at you with a different face every day. Above the living room are three pretty bedrooms with good beds, functional storage and windows south to the mountains or east to the fields behind. One bathroom upstairs, a shower room downstairs and an excellent, fully-fitted kitchen complete the picture. You feel perfectly secluded and have your own garden space beside the lily pond, yet are free to share the pool and main garden with other guests and the attentive, highly civilised Furney family. It is a quiet and beautiful spot. *Badminton, tennis and croquet available. Long winter lets available at £600 per month (oil fired central heating).*

Sleeps: 6-7.
Price: €558-€1,755 (£350-£1,100).
Bedrooms: 1 double; 1 twin; 1 room with bunkbeds; 1 tiny single; shower & wc; bath & wc.

Booking details:
Michael & Christine Furney
Tel: +33 (0)5 62 08 21 45
Fax: +33 (0)5 62 08 21 45
E-mail: setzeres32@aol.com
Web: www.members.aol.com/setzeres32

Map no: 12

Le Grenier, Setzères, 32230 Marciac

In the same stupendous surroundings of fine old buildings, green garden and stunning views, the smaller of the Setzères cottages is in the old grain loft and a rustic outside staircase leads to its new yet typically gabled front door. The Furneys have done another excellent conversion here. The door opens onto four characterful old armchairs on an oriental carpet, with round table and English Windsor chairs beyond: a good space for four, with a window like a lens homing in on a slice of green country topped by snowy Pyrenean peaks. The neat, sky-lit kitchen, a mix of natural wood and blue tiles, gives onto this end of the room, and the bedrooms are off either side. The yellow and pink double is smallish but has its own basin and the pink-tinged twin room is larger; both are well lit, have good storage and share the well-finished white bathroom. A terrace area and a good patch of garden are private to Le Grenier. Otherwise guests share the whole wonderful space with other visitors. *Winter lets available at £400 per month.*

Sleeps: 4.
Price: €399-€957 (£250-£600).
Bedrooms: 1 double; 1 twin;
bathroom with bath, shower & wc.

Booking details:
Michael & Christine Furney
Tel: +33 (0)5 62 08 21 45
Fax: +33 (0)5 62 08 21 45
E-mail: setzeres32@aol.com
Web: www.members.aol.com/setzeres32

Les Rosiers, Domaine de Peyloubère, 32550 Pavie

Peyloubère is a dreamlike group of 200-year-old buildings around a rose garden in 35 acres of private parkland. There's a river, waterfall, lake and long, long walks across the fields; a pool, a barbecue and space for all; and a *manoir* that was hand-painted and inhabited by Italian 20th-century artist Mario Cavaglieri. Les Rosiers is on the ground floor of the old manor itself and the Martins' sensitive refurbishment goes perfectly with its piece of "genuine Cavaglieri": the vibrantly colourful ceiling of the brass-bedded double bedroom, originally the family dining room. The other feature is the monumental inglenook fireplace in the living room, large and light with white painted beams and walls washed with Strassevil chalk paint. Tall French windows lead out to the shady garden which includes the original well house, still in working order but safely secured. Children will love the secret summerhouse in the woods and the magical waterfall. Explore this unspoiled area in the heart of historic Gascony by foot or by bike.

Sleeps: 4.
Price: €558-€1,037 (£350-£650).
Bedrooms: 1 double; 1 room with bunkbeds; shower & wc.

Booking details:
Theresa & Ian Martin
Tel: +33 (0)5 62 05 74 97
Fax: +33 (0)5 62 05 75 39
E-mail: martin@peyloubere.com
Web: www.peyloubere.com

Map no: 12

Fermier, Domaine de Peyloubère, 32550 Pavie

Look out for hoopoes by your own private waterfall, fed by the River Gers which flows through the breathtakingly beautiful estate of this 17th-century manor. With 35 acres of lawns, Italian gardens (the legacy of Italian artist Mario Cavaglieri who lived here) and ancient woods, there's space to roam. You'll scarcely be aware of the guests in the two other rented cottages, or the English owners, Theresa and Ian. Peybloubère used to be a working farm and Fermier was the farmer's cottage: its original beamed inglenook fireplace still warms and welcomes in the living room. Furnishings are crisp and new, with attractive modern beech furniture, deep blue sofas and full-length curtains. There's a state-of-the-art kitchen in rosemary and sunflower colours, a Saint Hubert dresser and steps to a sunny downstairs double bedroom. French doors lead out to the patio by the large saltwater pool, and to the garden beyond. Enjoy the birdlife and views over the fields. Sample Armagnac, a dry, golden brandy for which the area is famous.

Sleeps: 6-8.
Price: €718-€1,356 (£450-£850).
Bedrooms: 2 twins; 2 doubles, 1 with own shower; bathroom; 2 wcs.

Booking details:
Theresa & Ian Martin
Tel: +33 (0)5 62 05 74 97
Fax: +33 (0)5 62 05 75 39
E-mail: martin@peyloubere.com
Web: www.peyloubere.com

Notre-Dame de Lorette, 31420 Alan

This remarkable place was a hospital for the poor for **200** years, fell into ruin and was rescued by an equally remarkable man, Christophe Ferry. Architectural historian, cabinetmaker, music-lover and original, Christophe bought it because it reminded him of Tuscany. He's restored the hospital and its chapel with religious respect and every year he runs a major music festival in the grand *salle des malades*. A holiday here is a unique experience for anyone passionate about history. Meditate or stroll in the ancient cloisters, or walk the golden stone corridors and remember the lame who hobbled here before you. But don't expect luxury or cosiness. Furniture, although often beautiful (and in some cases restored by Christophe) is minimalist, the atmosphere is austere, and furnishings basic. The kitchen, although small, is a gem: it's been lovingly restored using old bricks and tiles and Christophe has crafted wooden cabinets by hand. To cap it all, the nearby village of Alan is one of the prettiest in France.

Sleeps: 6-8.
Price: €310-€485.
Bedrooms: 1 twin with shower (suitable for wheelchair users); 1 room with bunkbeds & 2 singles; 1 double; 1 bathroom; wc.

Booking details:
Christophe Ferry
Tel: +33 (0)5 61 98 98 84
Fax: +33 (0)5 61 98 98 84
E-mail: lorette@notredamedelorette.com
Web: www.notredamedelorette.com

Map no: 12

Le Coin Fleuri, 46110 Carennac

The age and beauty of this stone cottage in its tiny village on a bluff above the Dordogne river take your breath away: the house is at least 300 years old — no-one knows exactly — and the village, clustered around a 10th-century Priory, dates back to Roman times. This really is a gem. Sit on the timbered veranda among the geraniums and watch the gentle goings-on of one of the loveliest villages in France, or stroll to the banks of the Dordogne river, great for swimming or canoeing. Bob, the English owner, bought the cottage as a ruin, and has preserved its quaint Quercian character inside and out. The large living/dining room/ kitchen, with whitewashed stone walls, is modestly but comfortably furnished, and unusual knick-knacks give it a personalised, homely feel. The bedrooms, in the old goatsheds below, have yellow or pink painted stone walls, carpeted or lino floors, and simple furniture. Carennac has two restaurants serving traditional regional cooking, a *boulodrome* and a tennis court.

Sleeps: 4.
Price: €287-€446 (£180-£280).
Bedrooms: 1 double with bathroom & wc; 1 twin with shower & wc.

Booking details:
Bob Wallman
Tel: +44 (0)161 440 8990
Fax: +44 (0)161 440 8990
E-mail: robert@wallmanr.freeserve.co.uk

Map no: 12

Le Petit Coin, Prouilhac, 46300 Gourdon

Sit on the stone steps among the geranium pots and chat to passing villagers while you top and tail beans for lunch. Most will be French and friendly and if you make the effort you'll soon feel part of this hamlet with its stunning honey-coloured stone houses with ancient tiled roofs. Many houses date back to the 13th century, as does the pretty church a few yards up the road; borrow the key from the owners of your cottage, who live next door. This affable couple, who also have a son and grandchild in the village, restored this farmer's cottage from a ruin after moving here over a decade ago. You won't find sophistication — floors are linoleum and there's plenty of pine — but the atmosphere is cosy, homely and welcoming. An ancient half-glazed door leads left into a functional kitchen with white formica units and right into the dining/living room with a high-beamed sloping ceiling which gives a feeling of space and light. Two *bâteaux lits* double up as beds or sofas, and upstairs there's a simple double under the gables.

Sleeps: 2-4.
Price: €255-€350 (£160-£220).
Bedrooms: 1 double with wc; 2 singles in living room; bathroom & wc downstairs.

Booking details:
Angela & Clifford Bishop
Tel: +33 (0)5 65 41 39 73
Fax: +33 (0)5 65 41 39 73

Map no: 12

Pouch, 46500 Rignac

Here you have a chance to get a taste of French farming life: cows and sheep trundle past the gate twice a day and the butcher and grocer bring their vans to the village several times a week. This lovely barn conversion is the only foreign-owned house in the village so you'll have ample opportunity to perfect your French. The orchard, lawn and pool behind are totally private and if you come in season you can feast on apples, walnuts, plums and grapes. Stone steps lead up to the living room which runs the length and width of the house, with a gabled beamed roof and a woodburner against an exposed stone wall. The feel is pure, clean and modern with a hint of Scandinavia. Colours are blue and cream and there are comfy, modern, Ikea-style sofas to flop into. The bedrooms downstairs are functional without being austere, with old beams, modern furnishings and rough plastered walls. There's plenty to see in the area, from Neolithic caves and rock paintings to famous Rocamadour. The area is wonderful for walking and cycling too.

Sleeps: 4.
Price: €535-€690.
Bedrooms: 2 twins; shared shower & wc; separate wc.

Booking details:
Gavin & Lillian Bell
Tel: +33 (0)5 65 33 66 84
Fax: +33 (0)5 65 33 71 31
E-mail: lilianbel@aol.com

Maison Lafeuille, Rueyres, 46120 Lacapelle-Marival

Michael and Clova fell in love with this extraordinary rambling 17th-century farmhouse while on their honeymoon in the 70s, sold their grand piano to buy it and haven't looked back. Passionately respectful of its history, they named the house after the family who'd lived here for generations, and they've meticulously preserved its pagoda-like roofs, blue-grey shutters and small turret windows — not a plumbing pipe or picture window in sight. Inside, vast oak beams, antique furniture and beautiful wide-plank wooden floors enhance the old-world atmosphere. Stage musical soirées in the large living room with upright piano, vast inglenook fireplace and ancient door leading to the *bolet*, a covered balcony, perfect for breakfasts and aperitifs. Simple bedrooms, with sloping beamed ceilings, allow flexible sleeping arrangements: many interconnect and one upstairs double is divided from the children's dormitory by a curtain. Eat in the field below the big pool. Butchers' and bakers' vans call once a week, and there are shops in nearby Thémines.

Sleeps: 8-14 + 2 babies.
Price: €718-€2,156 (£450-£1,350).
Bedrooms: 3 doubles, 1 with cot; 1 single/double with cot; dorm with 6 singles, ensuite wc; shower & wc; bathroom (ext. entrance only).

Booking details:
Michael & Clova Stinton
Tel: +44 (0)1865 556307
E-mail: michael.stinton@abingdon.org.uk
Web: www.maison-lafeuille.co.uk

Map no: 12

Les Etriers, Séniergues, 46240 Labastide Murat

Impeccable and lavish, this farmhouse feels more like a five-star hotel than a holiday home: no surprise to discover the owner is an architect. The solid chestnut floor and Quercy furniture, some of it antique, are so pristine they gleam, and the beds so luxurious you'll find it hard to drag yourself out of them. Bedrooms, mostly in pastels, have tie-back curtains, pretty cloth-clad side tables, and jugs and basins with dried flowers. American visitors in particular will like this house between the Lot and Dordogne rivers, with prehistoric caves, canoeing and historic towns like Rocamadour and La Roque-Gageac all nearby. You'll come here too for the space — there's a vast field behind the house, ideal for football or snoozing in the sun — and the magical views of Séniergues, including its 13th-century church, which you can enjoy from the south-facing stone terrace. Weekly vans bring bread, *saucisson* and meat to your door. *A busy road nearby makes it unsuitable for young children.*

Sleeps: 6.
Price: €287-€718 (£180-£450).
Bedrooms: 2 doubles; 1 twin;
2 showers & wc on ground floor.

Booking details:
Richard Stirrup
Tel: +44 (0)1254 56096
Fax: +44 (0)1254 691379
E-mail: richard.stirrup@btinternet.com

Le Poux del Mas, 46160 Carayac

No televisions here. You'll come to this old, old farmhouse to forget the 21st century — and probably the 20th too. Marc's family have owned the house for generations, but left it derelict for 50 years before Marc embarked on its restoration a few years ago. He's undertaken the task with unusual sensitivity, respecting both the fabric and the spirit of the ancient house. The original bare oak floorboards and inglenook fireplace remain in the huge, austere living room, as do the old wooden partition separating it from the kitchen/dining room and some of the hugest oak ceiling beams. You'll even see the original pig-salting chest and, in an alcove, a stone 'long drop' (or privy), a remnant of the time when the gentry used this as a hunting lodge (only the gentry enjoyed such luxuries). Bedrooms, decorated in guileless patterned country wallpaper, are basic but adequate. Even the views over fields and woods are much as they must have been for generations, and the only thing to pass your door will be the sheep. Deeply special.

Sleeps: 7-8.
Price: €190-€440.
Bedrooms: 2 doubles, 1 with extra single; 1 twin; 1 single; shower & wc.

Booking details:
Marc Labarthe
Tel: +33 (0)5 65 40 00 90

Pech Grizou, Le Bougayrou, 46200 Lacave

Kyle, the artist owner, has tape-recorded 92 species of birds within a one-mile radius of this old, old stone cottage. If you're lucky, you'll spot peregrines, short-toed eagles and myriad species of wild orchids. The bucolic setting and Kyle's sensitive conversion leave you imagining you're still in pre-war, provincial, peasant France. Unaffected, and rustic, but perfectly comfortable, this cottage built into the rock exudes authenticity. There are well-loved leather armchairs and grandfather clock cases in front of the woodburner in the living room — warm your soup here in winter and the original stone sink is set into the wall. There's a comfortable, friendly kitchen with hardwood cupboard doors, and the bedroom under the rafters, nicely furnished with antiques, is blissfully cosy for a couple. There's excellent walking along the river Ouysse with its limestone cliffs, and canoeing on the Dordogne. Don't miss the pretty village of Belcastel, perched on a rock overlooking the great river. *Owner not resident.*

Sleeps: 2.
Price: €239-€439 (£150-275).
Bedrooms: 1 double with shower & wc.

Booking details:
Kyle Turner
Tel: +44 (0)1747 811464
E-mail: kyleturner@waitrose.com

Le Pesquier, La Toulzanie, 46330 Saint Martin-Labouval

Holiday in a cave — well almost. Built into the cliff on the site of an ancient troglodytic dwelling, this old, old house still has bare rock walls on one side which will keep you blissfully cool on roasting summer days. Come here to enjoy peaceful views of the village rooftops and the river Lot, and magical calm. The house — derelict for 40 years, and eight years in careful restoration — is the last in a row of five, the other four of which have been turned into one, and are infrequently visited by their friendly Parisian owners. Out of season, at least, you'll have the place to yourself. Choose your front door — there are three — and delight in the pleasing simplicity of the inside of this unusual house. The less rugged walls of the living room are cool duck-egg green, complemented by sky-blue rugs and armchairs and the original medieval sink inset into the wall. Bedrooms, plain and light, have a Nordic feel. Eat on the shady terrace, in the kitchen or, if it's cool, in the *porcherie* (pigsty) next door.

Sleeps: 2-5.
Price: €279-€597 (£175-£375).
Bedrooms: 2 doubles, 1 with shower & wc; 1 single; bathroom & wc.

Booking details:
Mark Stonebanks
Tel: +44 (0)207 681 7750
E-mail: mark.stonebanks@blueyonder.co.uk

Map no: 12

Lagardelle, 46800 Sainte Croix, Montcuq

"It's like Britain 50 years ago — unthreatened birds and flowers, virtually no cars or concrete, and lots and lots of space". This line from the brochure gives you a taste of what to expect when you arrive at this fabulous 17th-century stone barn surrounded by lavender and sunflower fields. It gives you an idea, too, of the infectious enthusiasm of its nature-loving and informed owners, Ben and Susanna, who live next door with their teenage daughter. If you want to walk, you're in good hands, as Ben (ex-Navy) runs walking holidays and knows the Quercy Blanc intimately. The couple have converted the barn with religious respect for original materials and structures (they resisted the temptation to enlarge the original small upstairs windows, for example). Clean wooden floors and white and stone walls create a mood of calm simplicity. Engravings in the sitting room depict the various ports Ben has sailed into, and there's a welcoming woodburner for cooler evenings. Visit pretty nearby Montcuq, or flop by the pool.

Sleeps: 5.
Price: €319-€1,109 (£200-£695).
Bedrooms: 1 double; 1 twin; 1 single; bathroom; wc.

Booking details:
Ben & Susanna Hawkins
Tel: +33 (0)5 65 31 96 72
Fax: +33 (0)5 65 31 81 27
E-mail: hawkinsben@aol.com

Map no: 12

120

La Chave, Pechpeyroux, 46170 Cézac

Lindy and Tony found a rare jewel here: a farmhouse untouched for over a century. Inhabited, when they bought it, by a bachelor French farmer who still cooked his stews over the open fire, the house has many of its original 1880s features. Working wells and an old bread oven still stand in the large garden, and in the outbuildings you'll spot the wires where leaves of tobacco — the farm's main crop — were hung to dry. Lindy, who also runs a (Sawday) B&B in the UK, clearly has a flair for decoration and has produced a stunning result: rooms are painted in soothing greens and creams, and furnished with period country pieces, many brought over from England, and have sanded floors with colourful kilims. There's a friendly, ever-so-modern kitchen, and a comfy sitting room with a woodburner which makes the house ideal in winter as well as in summer. Look out for the handsome French walnut *armoire* and the antique quilt in one of the cool bedrooms. *10% discount for fortnightly bookings. Special off-season rates for two to four people.*

Sleeps: 10.
Price: €956-€1,912 (£600-£1,200).
Bedrooms: 2 doubles, 1 with own bathroom & wc; 3 twins; 1 bathroom & wc; 2 showers & wc.

Booking details:
Lindy & Tony Ball
Tel: +44 (0)1725 518768
Fax: +44 (0)1725 518380

L'Oustal Nebe, 46170 Saint Alauzie

The views... Long, lazy and ever-changing vistas of rolling hills, fields and distant hamlets are a constant delight here. Revel in them from your private lawn, or from the attractive pot-filled veranda which runs the length of the pretty stone house. Despite its name (*L'Oustal Nebe* means 'new place' in Occitan), this was an ancient farm outbuilding, and has been cleverly converted by Dawn, the friendly English owner, who lives next door. An interior designer in a previous life, Dawn has furnished the house like a home, with interesting knick-knacks, pot plants and even a sewing machine! His and Hers golf clubs are provided too, if you're interested, together with membership of the local golf club which also has tennis courts and a swimming pool. The welcoming kitchen/living room has a quarry-tiled floor, a fine inglenook fireplace with a wood-burner, and warm old oak beams. The simple, light bedrooms — one with a four-poster — have stripped pine furniture, tiled floors and sublime views. Walk in the woods, or visit nearby Montcuq and Lauzerte.

Sleeps: 4-5.
Price: €489-€897 (£300-£550).
Bedrooms: 2 doubles/twins, 1 with extra single, 1 with cot; bathroom & wc.

Booking details:
Dawn Lyde
Tel: +33 (0)5 65 22 98 57
Fax: +33 (0)5 65 22 98 57
E-mail: loustalnebe@aol.com
Web: www.loustalnebe.com

Map no: 12

Bicary, 81600 Broze

The Gaillac region is famous for its powerful, spicy red wines — locals claim they were made here even before the Roman conquest — and a green sea of vines surrounds this lovely 18th-century *domaine*. The nearest *cave* for wine-tasting is a short stroll away; and you might splash out on a special vintage to accompany one of the exquisite dinners which British owner Suzie will cook for you if you ask in advance. She, ex-publishing, and Robert, once a radio presenter for Classic FM, live with their two children in the main house next door. This converted two-storey stone barn can be rented as two small apartments or as one family-size one: ideal for two couples holidaying together, or a couple with a child and nanny. Stylish, light and spotless, each apartment has pine floors, exposed beams and generous windows overlooking the gardens and fruit orchards. Bedrooms are on a mezzanine level and each apartment has a private terrace. Aesthetes and athletes alike will love it here: paint, walk, canoe, or enjoy the Toulouse Lautrec collection at Albi.

Sleeps: 2-3 or 4-6.
Price: Each apt: €230-€740.
Bedrooms: Each apartment: 1 double plus sofabed; bathroom & wc.

Booking details:
Suzie & Robert Booth
Tel: +33 (0)5 63 57 48 65
Fax: +33 (0)5 63 57 48 65
E-mail: robert.booth@free.fr

Map no: 12

Château de Mayragues, 81140 Castelnau de Montmiral

Superlatives don't exist to describe this remarkable cottage in its château grounds. It has everything: history, vineyards, atmosphere. The château, vast and mellow, is 14th-century and, with its overhanging balcony circling the upper storey, is an outstanding example of the region's fortified architecture. Its immaculate and authentic restoration over eight years won French-born Laurence and her Scottish husband Alan a national prize. Your home is the château's old bread oven, with its own south-facing terrace where you can relax over a glass of their organic wines. It's simply but pleasingly furnished inside, cosy but light. There's a kitchen/living room with dark wooden floorboards and a mix of antique and new furniture, while the bedroom has a blue and white theme with pretty checked curtains. Look out onto the 17th-century *pigeonnier* 'on legs'. If you ever tire of just being here, there's walking country all around, and the nearby medieval hilltop village of Castelnau de Montmiral is well worth a visit.

Sleeps: 2-3.
Price: €305-€381.
Bedrooms: 1 double plus single bed; shower & wc.

Booking details:
Alan & Laurence Geddes
Tel: +33 (0)5 63 33 94 08
Fax: +33 (0)5 63 33 98 10
E-mail: geddes@chateau-de-mayragues.com
Web: www.chateau-de-mayragues.com

Le Pigeonnier, Le Pradet, 81170 Le Riols

Children will love this ancient *pigeonnier*, its large, luxuriant gardens, and the friendly welcome radiated by Dutch owners Marja and Ben. The multi-lingual couple live with their three young boys in the other half of this converted farmhouse, and will be happy to recommend *bastide* villages to visit and places to canoe or walk. Interior decoration is simple verging on spartan, creating a feeling of light and space. Ancient beams blend comfortably with pale wooden floors and white painted chairs in the large kitchen/dining room. There's a dining table here, but on lazy summer days you're more likely to eat under the vine-covered pergola overlooking the garden and pool. There are pleasant reproduction antiques in the carpeted double bedroom on the ground floor, and a steep pine staircase leads from the kitchen to a children's twin with wooden floors and wonderful views. Explore the remote and beautiful hills of Rouergue or walk the cobbled lanes of medieval Cordes which, although touristy, is fascinating. Good family value.

Sleeps: 4.
Price: €300-€600.
Bedrooms: 1 double downstairs;
1 twin/double upstairs; shower & wc
on ground floor.

Booking details:
Ben Demmer
Tel: +33 (0)5 63 65 48 18
E-mail: pradet@club-internet.fr

  Map no: 12

Les Devezes, 81190 Mirandol

History oozes from this labyrinthine 18th-century stone farmstead with its enclosed central courtyard. Here are ancient wooden wine vats, a solid stone bread oven and an old forge — now a kiln where Gloria, one of the spirited British owners, fires her pots. She and Elizabeth, ardent Francophiles both, live in the central section of the building and will probably invite you in for drinks if you want to be sociable (but will happily leave you alone if you don't). The cottage, in the south-east wing, has its own private entrance from a second enclosed courtyard. Geranium-decked steps lead to a large living room with exposed stone walls and a wide traditional hearth with a woodburner and a kitchen off one end. A locally-made ash staircase leads up to two cosy twin bedrooms under the eaves. One is the old *pigeonnier* which still has a carved three-hole stone alcove for the birds; the other has a dormer window looking onto the rooftops and the central courtyard. Swim in the pool in the large garden or in the Viaur river nearby.

Sleeps: 6.
Price: €558-€1,316 (£350-£825).
Bedrooms: 1 double; 2 twins; bathroom & wc.

Booking details:
Gloria Budgen
Tel: +33 (0)5 63 76 98 28
Fax: +33 (0)5 63 76 98 28

Château de Fourès, 81170 Campes/Cordes

Swap stress for bliss at this gem of a cottage in the grounds of a 19th-century château. You'll be hard put to decide what to do first: stroll across the estate, relax by waterlily-filled ponds, visit historic Cordes (two kilometres away), change into your whites for a game on your (private) tennis court, or drink in the peace and views from the roof terrace. The cottage has been beautifully restored by Madeleine, from Paris, and her Swiss husband Peter, who settled here after years of working abroad. They will respect your privacy but provide help when you need it. Furnishings are high quality, furniture is antique, the atmosphere attractive and light-filled. There are terracotta floors, beamed ceilings and warm-coloured throws and rugs. Eat at the round table in the stunning, wooden fitted kitchen, or outside on the shingled patio with its colourful flower beds. The light upstairs bedroom has wooden floorboards, pretty lace bedcovers and a door leading onto the roof terrace. Worth every Euro.

Sleeps: 4.
Price: €550-€800.
Bedrooms: 1 double; shower & wc downstairs; 2 single sofabeds downstairs.

Booking details:
Madeleine Camenzind-Acory
Tel: +33 (0)5 63 56 13 55
Fax: +33 (0)5 63 56 13 55

　Map no: 13

Le Vergnet, Canezac, 81190 Montirat

Hard to beat: an ancient stone farmhouse in an acre of grounds, a dreamy cottage garden and two wonderful owners. In spring you'll find orchids and cowslips, and in autumn wild mushrooms. Nightingales and hoopoes nest in the garden. The house has been restored from a virtual ruin by two charming and entertaining women, Gloria and Elizabeth, who have retained original materials wherever possible. An open-plan, quarry-tiled kitchen/dining room, equipped with Gloria's studio pottery, leads to a large bedroom in a converted outhouse, and the kitchen and the bedroom have doors onto the flagstoned terrace where you can eat in the shade of a vine pergola. The sitting room, in keeping with local tradition, is on the first floor and has a stone fireplace and the original hand-carved stone sink. Sit on the veranda and wallow in views of the Pyrenees or flop into the pool and listen to the birdsong. Visit Cordes and Castres or walk parts of the *Grande Randonnée des Gorges de Viaur* in an area famous for its wildlife and rugged beauty.

Sleeps: 6.
Price: €558-€1,476 (£350-£925).
Bedrooms: 1 double; 2 twins;
bathroom & wc.

Booking details:
Elizabeth Page & Gloria Budgen
Tel: +33 (0)5 63 76 98 28
Fax: +33 (0)5 63 76 98 28

Le Château, 81170 Noailles

Creaking studded doors, secret passages, majestic four-poster beds and bucketloads of atmosphere: everything's here in this fairytale castle. Built as a château-fort in the 13th century, it's been lived in for three generations by the Prouhet family who now live in the hamlet. Dine like princes and princesses in the vast vaulted dining room with its great brick-and-stone fireplace (the secret passage, to a small *salon*, is here), stone-flagged floors and a food cupboard which dates back to the 12th century. If you don't fancy cooking in the inglenook, return briefly to the 21st century in the well-equipped, newly renovated, vaulted kitchen, pretty with terracotta, blue and cream wall tiles, where you'll find all mod cons and a double oven. Wind your way up the stone staircase to the bedrooms with Renaissance coffered ceilings, lovely antique furniture, and views of the grounds. Rapunzels can retreat to the tiny bedroom in the turret. Sit out in your private garden and enjoy a glass of local wine. *Open May-October.*

Sleeps: 8-9.
Price: €381-€610.
Bedrooms: 1 double; 2 twins each with extra single bed, 1 with own bathroom & wc; 1 single; shower; wc.

Booking details:
Claire Prouhet
Tel: +33 (0)5 63 56 85 84
Fax: +33 (0)5 63 56 35 38
E-mail: clprouhet@club-internet.fr
Web: www.cordes-sur-ciel.org/pages/gite-chateau-de-noailles.htm

Map no: 13

La Grange, La Bastide, 81440 Lautrec

Rural, rambling and tranquil, this 17th-century farmstead has views which are hard to beat. On clear days you'll see the snowy peaks of the Pyrenees, and the property's four and a half hectares of meadows and woods are guaranteed to soothe the soul. You'll be infected with the friendly enthusiasm of Ian and Jos who retired here after 25 years running English country hotels, and who live on the edge of the estate. They've put their expertise to good use in converting this lovely stone barn and the neighbouring farmhouse and cottage which can also be rented. Old beams and stones have been retained, and furniture is a happy mix of antique and new. In the open-plan living room/kitchen you'll find deliciously high ceilings, rug-strewn polished wooden floors and inviting pink sofas. French windows lead out to a long iron-balustraded terrace overlooking the pool. Pick your spot in the gardens to dine out, or if you don't fancy cooking, Jos may agree to lay on one of her heavenly dinners. *Can be rented with farmhouse, sleeping total of 12-16, for £600-£2,100 per week.*

Sleeps: 4-6.
Price: €558-€1,276 (£350-800).
Bedrooms: 1 double; 1 twin with shower & wc; 1 double sofabed on mezzanine; bathroom & wc.

Booking details:
Ian & Jocelyn Bryant
Tel: +33 (0)5 63 70 56 96
Fax: +33 (0)5 63 70 56 96
E-mail: tarngites@aol.com
Web: www.tarn-gites.com

Map no: 13

Brezou Main House, 82140 Saint Antonin Noble Val

Follow in the steps of the stars: many have stayed here, which gives you some idea of the luxurious style of this gorgeous 1901 manor house. Owners Rod and Jayne and their young daughter Nicole live here most of the year so it feels like an exceedingly smart home rather than a rented property. With spectacular views, an acre of mature garden, an inviting (fenced) pool, and sumptuous furnishings, you'll want for nothing. If you are two or three families holidaying together, feast in the vast but welcoming open-plan kitchen/dining room with great oak beams and a long antique dining table and benches. The kitchen area, with soft yellow walls and pretty check curtains, is immaculately equipped, with plenty of beech work surfaces on which to prepare the goodies you've bought from the market (the Sunday one in Saint Antonin is a must). There's a comfortable sitting room and a well-stocked formal terracotta and white library too. *Only available July & August, let with Lodge House (see next page) as five-bedroom house.*

Sleeps: 6 (or 10 including Lodge House).
Price: €2,349-€2,827 (£1,475-£1,775) for both houses.
Bedrooms: 2 doubles, 1 with bathroom & wc; 1 twin; bathroom & wc.

Booking details:
Jayne & Rod Millard
Tel: +33 (0)5 63 30 68 89
Fax: +33 (0)5 63 68 23 60
E-mail: rod@brezou.com
Web: www.brezou.com

Map no: 12

Lodge House, 82140 Saint Antonin Noble Val

With its pretty blue shutters and soothing views, this hilltop gatehouse has been attractively restored by Rod and Jayne who moved here seven years ago to live the rural dream. They live in the main house across the courtyard (except in July and August, when the two houses are rented together) and are always happy to put themselves out for guests while respecting privacy. Sand-coloured walls, hung with interesting pictures, and terracotta tiled floors create a warm, cosy atmosphere in the kitchen/dining/living room which has huge oak beams and a wood-burner. Walk out from here into your small south-facing private garden where you can eat out or sit and enjoy the peace of this beautiful area. The long, narrow twin bedroom downstairs has pretty antiques, while the double upstairs has a navy and white colour scheme. Children will love the large (shared) gardens and pool, and the fenced play area with a climbing frame and paddling pool.

Sleeps: 4.
Price: €446-€558 (£280-£350).
Bedrooms: 1 double; 1 twin;
bathroom & wc.

Booking details:
Jayne & Rod Millard
Tel: +33 (0)5 63 30 68 89
Fax: +33 (0)5 63 68 23 60
E-mail: rod@brezou.com
Web: www.brezou.com

Map no: 12

Country Cottage, 82140 Saint Antonin Noble Val

Just a short drive away is rural, historic Saint Antonin Noble Val, a medieval town which clings to the banks of the Aveyron beneath towering white cliffs. The town's prosperity from manufacturing cloth and leather has left a stunning heritage of ancient houses which fan out from the lovely Place de la Halle, and the weekly market is unmissable. Surrounded by pasture and woodland, and with an acre of garden, this old stone farmhouse is a tranquil refuge. Drink in the serene views from the blue and white bedrooms upstairs with wooden floors and attractive rugs; downstairs, the fabulous double bedroom with antique furniture and luxurious linen has wooden doors leading to a terrace. The comfortable living room/kitchen has beams and exposed stone walls. Enjoy the birdsong from the large (fenced) pool in front of the house, or explore this ruggedly beautiful area on foot — GR footpaths abound. *Not available July or August.*

Sleeps: 6.
Price: €518-€836 (£325-£525).
Bedrooms: 2 doubles, 1 downstairs with own shower & wc; 1 twin; bathroom & wc.

Booking details:
Jayne & Rod Millard
Tel: +33 (0)5 63 30 68 89
Fax: +33 (0)5 63 68 23 60
E-mail: rod@brezou.com
Web: www.brezou.com

Terre Negre, 82150 Montaigu de Quercy

If the horse brasses above the fireplace remind you of an English country pub it's no coincidence, for Mark and Suzie used to run one in deepest Devon. The Anglo-Swedish couple moved here in search of an even quieter, more rustic life, and restored this Quercian farmstead in rolling countryside. Its name comes from the area's abundance of truffles, known locally as Black Gold. Your hardworking hosts are quietly friendly and live on the edge of the estate. Furnishings are budget, mostly pine and cane, and the old ceiling beams and exposed stone walls the only reminders of the house's great age — parts date back to 1650. The spotless master bedroom has a vaulted ceiling, cream walls and bedcovers and an attractive old wardrobe. Seek out your own secret corner of the large, colourful garden; although you share it with another rented cottage and with the owners, space and privacy are not a problem. Cool off in the pool or shop at the weekly market in Montaigu de Quercy.

Sleeps: 4.
Price: €360-€725.
Bedrooms: 1 double; 1 twin; shower & wc.

Booking details:
Suzie & Mark Robinson-Ball
Tel: +33 (0)5 63 94 43 86
Fax: +33 (0)5 63 94 43 86
E-mail: terrenegre@libertysurf.fr

Map no: 12

Auvergne

Photography by Michael Busselle.

Les Ris, Vilanciaux, 03350 Theneuille

Mooing cows may rouse you in the mornings, but otherwise you'll have total tranquillity in this 18th-century farmhouse. The cows are Salers — reddish-brown with huge horns — and their milk makes a magnificent cheese. You'll be given fresh eggs, milk and cheese on arrival by your lovely and unassuming hosts, Swiss-born Irène, who's an agronomist, and her Moroccan husband Hassan. They run the 80-hectare farm organically. The couple, who live just 500 metres away, will make you feel part of the family and children are welcome to look round, or even help on the farm. The décor is unsophisticated, with plenty of mass-produced pine furniture, but old beams have been kept and there's a woodburner in the sitting/dining room. There's a small patio where you can eat out. Use the house as a base from which to walk or cycle, or swim in the lakes of the massive Forêt Tronçais, which claims to be the largest oak forest in Europe. Ideal for a family wanting to experience rural life. Children will love it.

Sleeps: 6-7.
Price: €305.
Bedrooms: 1 twin with extra single bed; 1 twin; 1 double; shower; wc.

Booking details:
Irène & Hassan Benani
Tel: +33 (0)4 70 67 53 05
Fax: +33 (0)4 70 67 55 55
E-mail: benani@club-internet.fr
Web: perso.club-internet.fr/benani

Demeure d'Hauterive, 03340 La Ferté Hauterive

Sandwiched neatly between the Lefebvres' imposing *maison de maître* and the half-timbered tower of a medieval priory, this exquisite 19th-century guard's house is a delight. Walk from the kitchen door into three hectares of mature parkland, stroll into the village or just relax in the house's spotless and welcoming rooms. The cottage, and the big house next door where Annick and Jérôme run a B&B, had been empty for 30 years when the couple fell in love with them and bought them six years ago. They've restored the cottage with taste and style, furnishing it with family antiques including a wonderful grandfather clock and an oak dresser in the dining room. Old terracotta floors and beamed ceilings have been beautifully preserved as has the great stone fireplace. An oak staircase leads up to immaculate bedrooms with white bedcovers and delicate printed wallpapers. Look out for the paintings by members of the Lefebvre family. Be sure to eat at Les Muriers, the local restaurant, and to visit at least some of the Allier's 1,000 châteaux.

Sleeps: 8 + 1 baby.
Price: €430.
Bedrooms: 2 doubles; 1 twin, 1 bunk for three; cot in corridor; shower & wc; wc.

Booking details:
Annick & Jérôme Lefebvre
Tel: +33 (0)4 70 43 04 85
Fax: +33 (0)4 70 43 00 62
Web: www.demeure-hauterive.com

Longevialle, 15140 Saint Paul de Salers

Pack your hiking boots. Bang in the heart of the dramatic Plomb de Cantal, this newly converted barn will delight walkers and anyone who wants a glimpse of an area of rural France which has changed little in centuries. Nearby medieval (if touristy) Salers with its cobbled streets, gateways and turreted mansions crafted from the dark Auvergnat volcanic rock is another treat. Don't miss the weekly market where farmers sell delicious Cantal and other cheeses for which the area's lush pastures are famous. Although in the hamlet, the house feels totally private, and has south-facing views over a pleasant garden for *al fresco* dining. The downstairs is open-plan, with new pine floors and panelled walls which give a roomy, airy feel. The kitchen has one of the original stone walls, and the (absent) French owner thoughtfully leaves a selection of recipes for you. Spotless pine-clad bedrooms, one a mezzanine, have fabulous views. Walk from the door onto the GR400 *Tour du Cantal* footpath which takes in Puy Violent and Puy Mary. There's cross-country skiing in winter.

Sleeps: 6-8.
Price: €285-€520.
Bedrooms: 3 twins; double sofabed in living room; 2 showers; wc.

Booking details:
Mlle Marie-Geneviève Bauchant
Tel: +33 (0)2 47 29 50 70
E-mail: longevialle@multimania.com
Web: www.multimania.com/longevialle

Raymond, Mandailles St Julien, 15590 Aurillac

Walk straight out of this traditional Auvergnat house with its steely slate roofs into wonderful countryside. You can hear a gurgling stream from your bed and all around there are breathtaking views of the cone-shaped *puys*. The 200-year-old house used to be two cottages. One half retains the living room where once the family ate, lived and slept: it still has the original wooden beams, long table, and fireplace with seats where you can toast your toes and relax after a day's walking. The other half, a ruin when the Haines found it, has a modern feel, and extra windows have been added to make it light and airy. Bedrooms too are a blend of ancient (crannied and characterful) and modern; one leads to a terrace. Visit local cheesemakers to sample Cantal for which the area is famous, shower under the waterfall in the river, or visit the market in Aurillac. You can buy fresh milk, yogurt and goat's cheese from the farmer next door, and a travelling shop drives to the house three times a week — listen out for his horn.

Sleeps: 6.
Price: €380.
Bedrooms: 2 doubles, 1 with wc;
1 twin/double; 2 showers & wc.

Booking details:
Ann & Stephen Haine
Tel: +44 (0)207 267 8936
Fax: +44 (0)207 813 5573
E-mail: annhaine@compuserve.com

Map no: 13

Moulin de Cayrols, 15290 Cayrols

You're in a tiny Auvergnat village but once you arrive at this magical watery paradise in the woods you forget the outside world. The house, an 18th-century flour mill, has been restored by its Parisian owners with imagination and sensitivity. The downstairs, where millstones once creaked, combines kitchen, living and dining room and feels like the genuine family home it is. There are inviting well-used armchairs around a stone fireplace, plenty of ornaments and pictures and a modern oak table and chairs. Below in the old machine room is another large sitting room — ideal for children to play or sleep in. Recline in the huge ground-floor master bedroom and listen to the sound of cascading water. Whitewashed walls are hung with family portraits and doors lead to a balcony. Upstairs bedrooms are wood panelled, carpeted and decorated in vivid floral wallpaper. Children will love swimming in, or rowing on, the two lakes and exploring the streams and woods. There are good longer walks too. Great value. *Not suitable for very young children.*

Sleeps: 6.
Price: €410-€590.
Bedrooms: 1 twin; 2 doubles;
2 bathrooms with wcs.

Booking details:
Cecile Limont-Ivanoff
Tel: +33 (0)1 45 72 11 96
Fax: +33 (0)1 45 74 90 16
E-mail: MoulindeCayrols@aol.com

Map no: 13  139

Ferrières, La Chourlie, 15340 Senezergues

Come here for the great fish-scale, stone-tiled roof, the spectacular setting among the rolling hills of the Cantal, and to experience the peaceful life of a farming hamlet. This typical Auvergnat stone cottage, built in the 1820s, has been attractively modernised by British owners May and Maurice who live eight kilometres away and have a pool which you're welcome to use. Well used to wild, roaming countryside, they retired here after 17 years running a hotel on Dartmoor. The area is called La Châtaigneraie after its sweet-chestnut trees, a staple food since the middle ages; if you stay in October visit the annual chestnut fair. Inside, oak-beamed rooms are generous in comforts and rustic cosiness. In the dining/living room there's a large working *cantou* fireplace and a dining table Maurice has made from old roof timbers. An oak staircase leads up to wood-floored bedrooms with reproduction antique furniture and exposed stone walls. Relax in the large garden with a pre-dinner drink, then sample the Auvergne's wholesome cuisine in nearby village restaurants.

Sleeps: 6.
Price: €399-€757 (£250-£475).
Bedrooms: 1 double; 1 twin; 1 room with bunkbeds; bathroom/shower; wc; shower & wc downstairs.

Booking details:
May & Maurice Harbridge
Tel: +33 (0)4 71 49 24 87
Fax: +33 (0)4 71 49 24 87

Map no: 13

Sweet Little House, La Borie d'Estaules, 15190 Condat

Tiny, south-facing and built into the rock, this stone house is described by its owners as "dolls' house pretty". Di and her farmer husband Peter moved here from Devon in search of solitude and if you seek the same you'll love it. It was built a century ago for the haymaker and its slate roof (steeply sloped to fend off snow) is typical of the Auvergne. Materials are basic — there's plenty of pale pine — but Di has given it style through careful selection of furniture and furnishings. A set of antique copper pans decorates the compact kitchen, and there are a fine wrought-iron bed and some country antiques in the bedrooms upstairs. Rooms are uncluttered and immaculately clean, creating a feeling of light and space. The living room has parquet floors and a Godin woodburner, the walls are decorated with the farm implements used by the original haymaker. There's a tiny patio where you can eat out, and your gardens are the narcissi-filled meadows and the mountains of the Volcans d'Auvergne National Park. Bird watchers and walkers will love it.

Sleeps: 4.
Price: €383-€846 (£240-£530).
Bedrooms: 1 twin; 1 double with own wc and basin; bathroom & wc.

Booking details:
Di Scott
Tel: +33 (0)4 71 78 63 57
Fax: +33 (0)4 71 78 50 33
E-mail: scottcondat@compuserve.com
Web: www.auvergnehols.co.uk

Laquairie, 15190 Conduit

Neat, stylish and endearingly crooked, this lovely little house perched at 1,000m in the tiny hamlet of Laquairie (permanent population three families) is a real find. The living room has wonky walls and windows and a wonderful sloping wooden floor. British owners Di and Peter, who live 10 minutes' drive away, have restored this 100-year-old Auvergnat house immaculately, keeping original beams and fireplaces and adding comfy and elegant tables and chairs. There's a pretty downstairs single bedroom with an iron bedstead and new mattress, and the most crooked walls and window you've ever seen; upstairs there's a double with off-white walls and red and white *toile de Jouy* bedcovers. The three-foot-thick walls keep the house cool in the summer. The house is hard to beat if you like walking: you're in the heart of the Auvergne and have breathtaking views of the Rhue valley and the pointed, volcanic Sancy mountains in the distance. Historic Salers is nearby, and Conduit, with its lively Wednesday market, is five minutes by car.

Sleeps: 3.
Price: €415-€846 (£260-£530).
Bedrooms: 1 single; 1 double; shower room with wc and washing machine.

Booking details:
Di Scott
Tel: +33 (0)4 71 78 63 57
Fax: +33 (0)4 71 78 50 33
E-mail: scottcondat@compuserve.com
Web: www.auvergnehols.co.uk

Map no: 13

Les Fouesses, Sailles, 63710 Saint Nectaire

Perched on the rugged central spine of France known as the Massif Central, surrounded by the black protuberances of extinct volcanoes or *puys*, the views from this pretty cottage are hard to beat. There are snow-capped peaks in the distance, lush pastures all around and, on your doorstep, the lively village of Saint Nectaire, famous for its creamy cheese. The 18th-century three-storey house is typical of the Auvergne: built of volcanic stone with little windows and thick walls, it faces west to protect it from prevailing winds. Rooms are small and furnishings simple and functional. There's a small frilly twin bedroom on the first floor, and a larger attractive double with vaulted ceilings on the second. In summer you can spill out into the rose-decked private garden, and there's another bigger one if you don't mind sharing it with up to eight B&B guests who lodge in the house next door. Monique, your kind and enthusiastic hostess, can advise on anything and everything, from where to buy local cheese to the best walks in this wonderful region.

Sleeps: 4-5.
Price: €275-€335.
Bedrooms: 1 twin (with extra bed for child); 1 double; shower & wc downstairs.

Booking details:
Monique Deforge
Tel: +33 (0)4 73 88 40 08

Languedoc – Rousillon

Photography by Michael Busselle.

37 rue Notre Dame, 48320 Quezac

You are in forested mountain country, in the heart of the pretty medieval village of Quezac, and minutes from the magnificent Gorges du Tarn. Cycle, canoe, walk, or simply be — here is a quiet and comfortable base for lovers of the outdoors, well away from the holiday crowds. This stone village house is 17th-century but it has been completely modernised inside by its young and enthusiastic owners, Rémi and Françoise, who moved from Paris. They live next door and run a restaurant nearby. Built into the mountainside, the house is cleverly constructed on different levels. Clear, sharp lines dominate, and there's a light, minimalist feel. You'll find dormer windows, plenty of glass, and spanking new pine furniture. There's a large open plan living/dining room and kitchen overhung by a mezzanine bedroom; stairs lead to two more bedrooms below. Explore the gorge by bike (Rémi will rent you one), or on foot along the fabulous GR6a footpath between Le Rozier and Les Vignes.

Sleeps: 6-7.
Price: €350-€650.
Bedrooms: 1 twin; 1 double; 1 double plus single on mezzanine; shower & wc.

Booking details:
Rémi & Françoise Macon
Tel: +33 (0)4 66 44 22 99
Web: www.chez.com/quezac

La Filature, Roquedur le Haut, 30440 Sumène

A stunning and remote mountain area with a fascinating history and a house that marries eccentricity, style and comfort, and deep peace. If you're a nature lover, La Filature, in a hilltop village with a permanent population of 12, has it all. Its name, which literally means spinning mill, comes from the period when the silk industry boomed, and cocoons were unwound in hot water by the women of the house. Look out for the tell-tale tunnel of white mulberry trees — the silkworms' staple diet — on one of the many stone terraces which make up the large and attractive gardens. Enjoy cherries, greengages and apples from the fruit trees, or wander through the four-acre Spanish chestnut wood down to a stream. In autumn look out for truffles, mushrooms and wild boar. The old schist stone house has been beautifully restored and furnished by its (absent) English owners, with ancient oak beamed ceilings, colourful ethnic chair covers and wall hangings, and some lovely antiques. The views here on the edge of the Cévennes National Park are memorable. *Unsuitable for children.*

Sleeps: 6-10.
Price: €399-€718 (£250-£450).
Bedrooms: 2 doubles, both with extra single; 1 twin/double with bathroom & wc; 1 twin on mezzanine; shower & wc.

Booking details:
Carmela & Sebastian Pearson
Tel: +44 (0)1438 871364
Fax: +44 (0)1438 871921
E-mail: carmpears@aol.com

Map no: 13

La Maison Neuve, 30120 Breau et Salagosse

If you enjoy isolation, imaginative paintwork and unusual buildings, you'll love this ancient farmstead in the wilds of the Cévennes. Elizabeth and Paul bought it as a ruin after upping sticks with their four children and selling their British home. The layout is unusual: rooms lead off a central hall downstairs and from internal balconies on the upper floors. Stone by stone, Elizabeth and Paul, interior designers both, have tamed the building and its metre-thick walls, preserving original materials such as floor and roof tiles with passionate respect. Creaking nail-studded doors, gnarled roof beams and blackened stone fireplaces all remain. Elizabeth has made paint pigments to match the original bright colours, and applied them with rags to create a distressed look. Lovers of the outdoors will be in heaven too: there's mountain walking, donkey or horse-trekking, and swimming in the river. Or you can laze in the fruit orchards, or flop in the pool. In season, Elizabeth can sell you home-grown organic sweet onions and raspberries.

Sleeps: 12.
Price: €765-€2,135.
Bedrooms: 1 double with bathroom & wc; 2 doubles; 3 twins; 2 showers & wcs.

Booking details:
Elizabeth Adam & Paul Wellard
Tel: +33 (0)4 67 82 49 09
Fax: +33 (0)4 67 82 49 09
E-mail: betjeadam@aol.com

Map no: 13

146

La Mine d'Or, Les Oulettes, 30160 Gagnières

Dig in the river and you might find gold. This magical place at the foot of the Cévennes mountains was a gold mine until 1926 and you can see the pond where gold was washed and the bar where miners sipped *pastis* at the end of a long day. It later became a farm, and your snug cabin, cradled like a tree-house between great oaks, was once a pig sty. Swiss-born Rebecca, a massage therapist, and her French ex-dancer husband Didier now run the place as a retreat centre. Keen environmentalists, they are a serene and gentle pair and will welcome you to join other guests for a vegetarian dinner if you wish, but will respect your privacy if you prefer to commune with nature from your cabin. Drink in deep peace from your bedroom balcony with its views of mountains and the tumbling river. Inside, wooden walls and ceilings create the warm feel of a chalet in Rebecca's native Switzerland. There's an unusual outdoor kitchen on the terrace below, and a tiny sitting room with comfy chairs next door. A perfect love nest. *Summer only.*

Sleeps: 2.
Price: €200-€250.
Bedrooms: 1 double; shower & wc.

Booking details:
Didier & Rebecca Rouchon
Tel: +33 (0)4 66 03 14 29
Fax: +33 (0)4 66 03 14 29
E-mail: holynaturdays@club-internet.Fr

Map no: 13

Mas Mahistre, 30960 Saint Jean de Valeriscle

The ancient coal mine has long since been reclaimed by nature and this 200-year-old stone building which housed its boss now stands in splendid isolation in a sea of chestnut trees and conifers. Walk along the river to the medieval village of Saint Jean de Valeriscle, or stride straight onto the Cevenol hills for a magnificent day's walking. If you prefer to take it easy, flop by the pool among the eucalyptus trees, pluck cherries or plums from the orchard for your lunch, or read on the large terrace. The exterior betrays few of the delights that await inside: Gerda, the Flemish owner, is a painter and antique dealer, and has left her artistic stamp on the beautiful interiors. You'll see her paintings on the walls, and lovely antiques — most of them English — stand out against pristine walls in original olive greens, salmon pinks or yellows. Terracotta-tiled bedrooms have superb mountain views. You'll find it hard to leave. *A municipal swimming pool behind the house is open afternoons only in July & August.*

Sleeps: 10.
Price: €610-€915 (electricity extra).
Bedrooms: 2 doubles; 2 triples;
1 ground-floor bathroom; 2 showers;
2 wcs.

Booking details:
Gerda Vrydaghs
Tel: +33 (0)4 66 25 36 63
Fax: +33 (0)4 66 25 36 63

Mas de la Blaquière, 30140 Massillargues-Atuech

Silk, soap and *seigneurs* have moulded the history of this lovely honey-coloured 15th-century castle perched above the Gardon river. Exact details are few as the archives were destroyed by a servant with a grudge, but it is known that silkworms were bred here until markets collapsed, then soap was made until the outbreak of World War One. Today, wine keeps the château and the nearby hamlet going, and vineyards stretch out in all directions from the windows of your totally independent first-floor apartment. Large, light and beamed, it's been attractively furnished with polished antiques by the friendly Soubeiran family, who have lived here for generations. There's an open-plan living/dining room/kitchen downstairs, and wooden stairs lead up to a mezzanine-level bedroom, with a beautiful antique carved wardrobe and luxurious bed linen, and a further double. You have your own small garden and you can swim in the Gardon; pretty Anduze, famous for its pottery, is five kilometres away.

Sleeps: 4-6.
Price: €259-€381.
Bedrooms: 1 double on mezzanine with extra single bed; 1 double; 1 single downstairs; bathroom; wc.

Booking details:
Marie-Claude Soubeiran
Tel: +33 (0)4 66 83 42 81

Map no: 14

Les Trémières, 30580 Fons sur Lussan

This little jewel of a house used to be the village bakery and upstairs, nurtured by the warmth from below, silkworms were bred to make the silk for which this area was famous. It's just off the Place de l'Eglise of this pretty village, but it's blissfully quiet. Relax in the cottage garden overlooking fields behind, play the piano in the living room, or book yourself a yoga lesson with Marie or Robert next door. The couple had used the house for holidays for 30 years before moving here from Paris in search of a simpler life five years ago. They've restored it simply, giving it a homely rather than a sophisticated feel. Collections of antique irons and coffee grinders decorate the living/dining room/kitchen and there's an original washing plank by the old stone fireplace. Furniture is a mix of antique and modern, and the attic double bedroom has a sloping pine-clad ceiling and fitted carpet. Marie leaves home-made lavender soap, wine, flowers and other surprises for your arrival. Good swimming and canoeing in the nearby river Cèze.

Sleeps: 4.
Price: €200-€460 (heating extra).
Bedrooms: 1 double; 1 twin with own separate entrance; vaulted bathroom & wc.

Booking details:
Robert & Marie Freslon
Tel: +33 (0)4 66 72 93 16
Fax: +33 (0)4 66 72 93 16

Map no: 14

150

Les Bambous, 30131 Pujaut

The solemn chimes of the neighbouring church clock will lull you to sleep. This snug getaway for two has the advantage of being in the heart of an unspoilt Provençal village — it's a short walk to the baker's fresh croissants — and only 10 minutes from the centre of historic Avignon. At weekends you might witness a wedding in the *Mairie* around the corner and women still wash clothes in the village's stone *lavoir*. Michèle and Joël, who lodge B&B guests in their house next door, have done up this tiny space beautifully with exposed stone walls, beamed ceilings and terracotta floors. There's an old school desk and Joël's watercolours on the walls. The couple commissioned a well known ceramicist to make the bright buttercup-coloured tiles in the kitchen area and lovely navy and yellow tiles decorate the shower room. Cycle or walk in the hills around, strike out further to explore Avignon, or relax in your private garden under the shade of a horse chestnut tree. *Meals available in main house on request.*

Sleeps: 2.
Price: €260-€335.
Bedrooms: 1 double; shower room.

Booking details:
Joël & Michèle Rousseau
Tel: +33 (0)4 90 26 46 47
Fax: +33 (0)4 90 26 46 47
E-mail: rousseau.michele@wanadoo.fr

  Map no: 14

Haut Village, 30700 Vallabrix

It's virtually impossible to photograph this stunning village house, sandwiched between the other buildings of enchanting Vallabrix. Its old honey-coloured stones embrace its own private courtyard and pool, and there are countless delights: delicious views across the terracotta rooftops to distant hills, relaxation and privacy in a geranium-filled courtyard, and an interior among the best we've seen. It's been beautifully restored by English owners Sheila and John (they won't be here when you are) and each has left their personal stamp on the décor. You'll find original African paintings and wooden artefacts collected by him on business assignments, and stylish soft furnishings crafted by Sheila. The L-shaped three-storey house has a bedroom and bathroom downstairs; a vast dining/living room/kitchen with pastel yellow walls leads out to the terrace on the middle floor; on the top level are attractive bedrooms with tiled floors and old pine furniture. Visit ancient Uzès with its famous Saturday market.

Sleeps: 8-10.
Price: €2,393 (£1,500).
Bedrooms: 2 doubles with own bathroom & wc; 2 twins; 1 double; bathroom & wc; poolside shower & wc.

Booking details:
Sheila Owen-Smith
Tel: +44 (0)1483 894104
Fax: +44 (0)1483 894569

Map no: 14

Le Mas de James, 30580 Lussan

Music or videos, if you wish, will lull you to sleep; luxuriously crisp white sheets will ensure the sweetest dreams; and in the morning a monsoon-like shower will prepare you for another day in this blissfully beautiful part of southern France. Luxury and sophistication are the keynotes here, and British owners Julie and John, who live across the courtyard, have clearly spared no expense to make this converted farmhouse as near perfection as possible. The interconnected dining/living rooms and kitchen have a fresh, roomy feel, with sand-coloured stone floors and pastel-painted walls hung with framed prints and gilded mirrors. The bedrooms, each with their own entrance and private bathroom, have terracotta tiled floors and exposed stone or cool blue, rag-roll painted walls. The painted furniture was decorated by an artist from Toulouse — look out for the dolphins on one of the bedheads — and even the cast-iron baths are prettily stencilled. Eat out on your private terrace, or by the huge heated pool amid manicured lawns.

Sleeps: 8.
Price: €650-€2,665.
Bedrooms: 2 twins; 2 king-size doubles; all with own bathroom & wc.

Booking details:
John & Julie Milligan
Tel: +33 (0)4 66 72 91 57
Fax: +33 (0)4 66 72 91 57
E-mail: Mjohn11947@aol.com

Map no: 14

Le Rocher Pointu, 30390 Aramon

It's easy to understand why André and Annie (whose ancestors were English) decided to cut their ties with Paris and move to this 150-year-old stone *bergerie*. Although bustling Avignon is just 15 minutes away, it's wonderfully secluded here: a haven of peace and space, reached via a windy track through pine scrub. There's a field with a donkey in front, and a vast thumb of rock behind, which gives the place its name. The apartment is the furthest of four which have been recently added to the main house, ideal for several couples travelling together. Smart, small, compact, with old beams, Provençal tiles and some good antique furniture, it has a tiny well-equipped kitchen off the dining/sitting room, and a split-level bedroom with a single bed on the top level and a double below. Relax on the terrace among the lavender and olive trees and watch the sunset over the mountains, or dip into the lovely pool with its distant views of Mont Ventoux. *Also B&B. Washing machine shared with other apartments.*

Sleeps: 2 + 1 child.
Price: €640 (€720 for 3).
Bedrooms: 1 double; 1 single on mezzanine; shower & wc.

Booking details:
Annie & André Malek
Tel: +33 (0) 4 66 57 41 87
Fax: +33 (0) 4 66 57 01 77
E-mail: amk@rocherpointu.com
Web: www.rocherpointu.com

L'Auzonnet, Hameau de Meilhen, 30960 Les Mages

From the street you have no inkling of this hidden jewel. It's reached via a long stone tunnel and a cool hydrangea-filled courtyard above what used to be stables and pigpens, and has been converted with style by the delightful owners Sophie, who is French and worked for the BBC, and her English husband David, an artist and keen saxophonist. Sophie's passion is trawling flea markets and you'll enjoy the fruits of her labours, from old doors to antique prints and mirrors and ironwork lamps. The Wedgwood blue and white bedroom, with wonderful old beams, has a pretty shower room decorated with blue and white tiles and mosaics. There's another surprise behind the house: walk through the courtyard into a vast garden (with pool) that slopes down to the Auzonnet river where, if you are lucky, you'll spot kingfishers and herons. You can fish too. This is the edge of the Cévennes National Park, with rugged mountains to walk and streams to swim in; to the north are the Gorges de l'Ardèche. *Not suitable for young children or the infirm.*

Sleeps: 2-4.
Price: €399-€511 (£250-£320).
Bedrooms: 1 double with shower, wc;
2 single sofabeds downstairs.

Booking details:
Sophie Tinnams
Tel: +33 (0)4 66 25 66 26
E-mail: sophie.tinnams@wanadoo.fr

　　Map no: 14

La Bergerie, Pont du Gard, 30210 Remoulins

The setting — six hectares of woodland stretching down to the Roman Pont du Gard aqueduct — is breathtaking. Sit by the river and marvel at this feat of engineering while watching for birds of prey, some introduced by the previous owner when the estate was a bird reserve. Gérard, the owner, is a delight: hospitality runs in his veins and as likely as not he'll invite you to an impromptu dinner or show you his collection of hats. He's even created a gym by the pool where you can work off any extra pounds gained in the area's fine restaurants. This century-old sheepfold has been restored with minimalist elegance. Modern ironwork and antique furniture sit comfortably side by side in the sitting room/kitchen, while cream-rendered walls and quarry-tiled floors create a feeling of space and light. A futuristic metal staircase leads up to the carpeted bedrooms, one of which has a four-poster. Eat on your terrace overlooking the private vineyard. You'll share the grounds and pool with B&B guests and occupants of another cottage, but there's plenty of space.

Sleeps: 4-6.
Price: €770-€850.
Bedrooms: 1 double; 1 twin; double sofabed in living room; bathroom & wc.

Booking details:
Gérard Cristini
Tel: +33 (0)4 66 37 19 45
Fax: +33 (0)4 66 37 19 45
Web: www.laterredeslauriers.com

Map no: 14

156

Maison Danton, 34420 Villeneuve-lès-Béziers

The best way to reach this enchanting, tiny, blue-shuttered house is by barge, for it stands near the banks of the 240-kilometre-long Canal du Midi. You will be following in the wake of boat and barge owners who, for over 320 years, have been navigating this beautiful waterway linking the Atlantic and Mediterranean seas. However you get here, you'll enjoy the canal as a picnic spot or place to stroll, particularly in spring when its tree-lined banks are bright with yellow irises and wild gladioli. In a quiet corner of a pretty wine village, the little medieval three-storey cottage has been stylishly restored by Australian owner Jennifer-Jane, who runs a (Sawdays) B&B in a nearby street. There's a jaunty living room/kitchen with simple furnishings in oranges and turquoises (even the washing-up bowl is co-ordinated), set off by the pure white walls. Original 'saracen' spiral stairs lead up to a large bedroom, light and lacy, with honey-coloured walls and dreamy drapes. There's a study/storeroom on the floor above. Small, perfect, compact.

Sleeps: 2.
Price: €230-€350.
Bedrooms: 1 double; shower & wc.

Booking details:
Jennifer-Jane Viner
Tel: +33 (0)4 67 39 87 15
Fax: +33 (0)4 67 32 00 95
E-mail: anges-gardiens@wanadoo.fr

　Map no: 13

La Tour, Château de Grézan, 34480 Laurens

La Tour is just inside the castle gate, by the pool, and its kitchen and bathroom actually fit within a circular tower. The antique-style oval windows and the 'arrow-slits' let in limited light from the outside world, but with great beams and old, old stones it's more atmospheric than gloomy; blessedly cool in high summer. A floral sofa and a couple of deep easy chairs still leave plenty of space on the tiled ground floor for a generous country table and a great carved *armoire* containing the crockery. To one side is the double bedroom with its orange-curtained bed and window opening onto the vines. The twin room, behind a curtain on the mezzanine, gets air and light from the entrance hall and faces the old-fashioned bathroom in the tower at the other end of the gallery. An astonishing, wildly romantic castle setting, with a pool beneath the palms and a restaurant in the ramparts. *As Mme Lanson does B&B and has another cottage, you share the grounds in high season with up to nine others.*

Sleeps: 4.
Price: €400-€820.
Bedrooms: 1 double; 1 twin on
mezzanine; shared bathroom & wc
(inside the tower!).

Booking details:
Marie-France Lanson
Tel: +33 (0)4 67 90 28 03
Fax: +33 (0)4 67 90 05 03
E-mail: chateau-grezan.lanson@wanadoo.fr

Les Meneaux, Château de Grézan, 34480 Laurens

Enter the battlemented gateway in the 'medieval' castle walls (those turrets are 19th-century follies), cross the cobbled yard, and climb the old stone stairs. Les Meneaux feels big and somehow modern — yards of lovely, wide, original floorboards, high rafters, white walls and a fully-equipped kitchen that is definitely 1990s. The flat is big, light and uncluttered, its paintwork picked out in blue, its sideboard full of perfectly chosen china. It has simple country furnishings, a pretty blue triple bedroom, a smaller, spring-flowered twin and a sixth bed up on the mezzanine beneath the roof window. Outside the castle walls is the swimming pool, protected by palm trees and bamboo, where you can relax and eat, and beyond, a sea of vines beneath the great Languedoc sky. The garden, a superb mixture of wild and formal, has some fascinating native species and you can buy estate Faugères wine on the spot. *Mme Lanson also does B&B for six and there's another cottage, so there may be others sharing the grounds.*

Sleeps: 6.
Price: €515-€1,050.
Bedrooms: 1 twin, 1 double; 2 singles on mezzanine; bathroom & wc.

Booking details:
Marie-France Lanson
Tel: +33 (0)4 67 90 28 03
Fax: +33 (0)4 67 90 05 03
E-mail: chateau-grezan.lanson@wanadoo.fr

Map no: 13

La Vigne, Hameau de Cazo, 34360 Saint-Chinian

Simple and quietly elegant, this little pink village house will delight those who eschew fussiness and clutter. And the dreamy views of vineyards and the red-earthed hills of the Montagne Noire clear the mind, too. In a small working hamlet, the three storey house has been beautifully restored by Dutch owners Monique and Reinoud, who live in the next village. Neat box trees flank the front door and, inside, lovely original patterned Languedocian floor tiles are reinforced by clean white walls and simple furniture. Dine around the large farmhouse pine table, or outside among the almond trees and lavender in the inviting walled garden. In the simple double bedroom upstairs, colourful bedspreads and curtains draw out the rust-red hexagonal floor tiles. There's lots to explore in this little known corner of south-west France. Walk in the Montagne Noire and the Mont Caroux, swim in peaceful rivers, or drink in simple village life (with a glass of the local Minervois wine) while you watch sheep and goats lazily graze.

Sleeps: 4-5.
Price: €280-€570.
Bedrooms: 1 double; 1 twin suitable
for children, with extra bed;
bathroom; wc.

Booking details:
Monique & Reinoud Weggelaar
Tel: +33 (0)4 67 38 20 33
Fax: +33 (0)4 67 38 20 33
E-mail: monique.degenaar@worldonline.fr
Web: www.perso.worldonline.fr/monirein

Map no: 13

Paradix, 34440 Nissan-lez-Ensérune

The handsome gateway is 19th-century and the colourful garden traditional French in inspiration, but the designer interiors are resolutely modern: old and new coexist effortlessly in this collection of four apartments and a studio. This was once the *maison de maître* of a wine merchant — you'll see vines all around. The stables and outbuildings were imaginatively transformed into apartments by British architect Colin and his Swiss wife, Susanna, who previously ran a small hotel in Tuscany. Apartments have two storeys and a small patio garden; keynotes inside are light, space and clear lines. The look is strictly minimalist with the occasional colourful cushion or Matisse print contrasting with the pristine white walls and pale-pink floor tiles. Apartment One, the only home for four, has a large living/dining room with plenty of space to sit and read or enjoy the view of the stunning shrubbery outside which keeps each apartment private. A yellow spiral staircase leads up to the luxurious but stylishly simple bedrooms.

Apartment: 1.
Sleeps: 4.
Price: €720-€880.
Bedrooms: 2 doubles, each with shower & wc.

Booking details:
Susanna, Colin & Yvonne Glennie
Tel: +33 (0)4 67 37 63 28
Fax: +33 (0)4 67 37 63 72
E-mail: glennieauparadix@wanadoo.fr

Apartments Two, Three and Four, Paradix

You can tell from the beautiful blue and white apartment kitchens that Colin Glennie was once a professional chef: they're so well equipped that even the most faint-hearted cook will be inspired. All is perfection in apartments Two, Three and Four, the interiors a serene symphony of light woods and natural fabrics. Study, read or relax in the large, light living/dining rooms, or use the apartments as a base from which to visit Béziers (don't miss the riotous four-day *feria* in August), the Oppidum d'Ensérune, the nearby site of a 2,600-year-old Gallo-Roman settlement, and the Canal du Midi, with its colourful barges. If you don't fancy travelling, swim in the generously-sized pool or stroll among the roses and oleander in the huge garden. If you want a cheaper option, there's a lovely first-floor studio for two, where striking blues and reds are offset by white walls. Come to Paradix if you're seeking a week of minimalist perfection in discreet and beautiful surroundings. *Perhaps not suitable for young children.*

Apartments: 2 & 3.
Sleeps: Each apt. sleeps 2.
Price: €570-€720.
Bedrooms: 1 double with shower
room & wc.

Apartment: 4.
Sleeps: 2.
Price: €475-€610.
Bedrooms: 1 double with shower
room & wc.

Map no: 13   162 & 3

Bergerie de Lavagnac, 34530 Montagnac

Wander among evocative wooden sculptures in the secret garden behind these 18th-century farm buildings, once part of a sheep farm belonging to the Château de Lavagnac. If you feel sociable, join other guests in the large courtyard and enjoy views of the Cévennes mountains and the Hérault valley; cool off under an outside shower surrounded by natural stone; or chat in the communal outdoor kitchen as you prepare dinner. You can choose between privacy or conviviality at this six-acre farm and vineyard, beautifully transformed into self-catering rooms and apartments. German owner Rosa, a teacher from Berlin, wanted to create a friendly, multi-national base and you'll find a rich mix of cultures; stay here and study French or use the farm as a base to visit the sea or lovely medieval villages like Pézenas, the home town of Molière. Rooms share a kitchen, while the mezzanine studio and the apartment have their own. The latter (pictured below) has pretty exposed stone walls, attractive antiques and striking views from the terrace over the vineyards. (Details and prices for rooms & studio on request.)

Sleeps: Apt: 4-5.
Price: Apt: €500.
Bedrooms: 1 double; 2 singles, 1 with extra pull-out bed; shower & wc.

Booking details:
Rosa Fichna
Tel: +33 (0)4 67 24 07 49
Fax: +33 (0)4 67 24 07 49
E-mail: rosamail@club-internet.fr
Web: www.bergerie-de-lavagnac.de

Map no: 13

Les Vailhes, 34700 Lodève

Stay here for the lake: swim in it, sail on it, or sit on your vast vine-covered terrace and savour its ever-changing beauty. This simple farmhouse, in a hamlet perched on its shores, is ideal for groups or two families who enjoy the outdoor life. If water's not your thing, there are riding stables nearby, you can hire mountain bikes, and the walking is superb. The house has been restored by Aline and Didier, an 'alternative', friendly young couple who farm sheep organically and live in the house next door. Inside décor is basic and minimalist, the black and white 1920s floor tiles and colourful ethnic-style curtains and bedcovers contrasting with pure white walls. The kitchen/dining room has pine cupboards and furniture and French doors out to the terrace; bedrooms are simple and uncluttered. Aline and Didier are also restoring the barn to make a big work room for groups. If you ever tire of just watching the water, you can canoe on the Hérault river, hike in the Monts de l'Espinouse, or visit old-fashioned Lodève with its famous Saturday market.

Sleeps: 13.
Price: €610-€762.
Bedrooms: 3 doubles; 1 triple;
1 dorm with four singles; 3 showers;
2 wcs.

Booking details:
Didier Brière & Aline Delfosse
Tel: +33 (0)4 67 44 43 80
Fax: +33 (0)4 67 44 43 80

Map no: 13

165

Domaine de Sicard, 11270 Ribouisse

Heaven for nature lovers: in spring you hear nightingales, the Pyrenees are on the doorstep and the farmhouse itself stands in 25 acres of woods and pasture. The Van Vliets abandoned successful careers in Holland to find a stress-free environment in which to bring up their daughter. She's now left home, but they still look after a dog, cats and a horse called Stix, and Wout devotes much of his time to drawing and painting. The charming and dynamic couple have renovated this ancient farmhouse stone by stone (the original supposedly dates from 1271) and turned half into a holiday cottage. On summer days, snooze in the garden among lilac trees, lavender and roses, or dine outside on the private terrace. Inside the house is immaculate and there's an exquisite new wood-beam ceiling in the living/dining room. Furnishings are modest but comfortable in authentic 1960s style, and bedrooms have wonderful views of the gardens and the mountains. The medieval towns of Mirepoix and Carcassonne are nearby, and there's horse-riding too. Great value.

Sleeps: 4.
Price: €259-€434.
Bedrooms: 1 double; 1 twin; shower & wc.

Booking details:
Wout Van Vliet
Tel: +33 (0)4 68 60 50 66
Fax: +33 (0)4 68 60 50 66
E-mail: domainesicard@hotmail.com

Map no: 12

Le Vieux Relais, 11700 Pépieux

In the 17th century it was a coaching station, today it's a haven of tranquillity in the heart of a bustling Languedoc wine-producing village. You're a stone's throw from the square where, daily, vans sell anything from lobsters to loo rolls and tractors roar past with their vinous loads. Retreat into the house and you'll forget the outside world. Sally, a British interior designer, has created a happy marriage of solid old French and modern inspiration. When there are no guests Sally lives here, so the house has a homely feel while also being stylishly luxurious. There's a large fitted kitchen, beautifully equipped (Sally's a professional cook, too) with a door to the pretty cobbled central courtyard where you can eat out. There's a formal dining room, a sitting room in greens and yellows, a ping-pong room and a reading room. Bedrooms are huge and sumptuous, mostly carpeted and furnished with pine or reproduction antiques. There's plenty to do, from wine-quaffing at the local *caves*, to visiting the Canal du Midi and historic Carcassonne.

Sleeps: 11.
Price: €1,276-€3,031 (£800-£1,900).
Bedrooms: 2 doubles with bathroom
& wc; 1 twin with bathroom & wc;
1 double; 1 single; shower & wc.

Booking details:
Sally Worthington
Tel: +33 (0)4 68 91 69 29
Fax: +33 (0)4 68 91 65 49
E-mail: sally.worthington@wanadoo.fr
Web: perso.wanadoo.fr/carrefourbedbreakfast

Map no: 13

Lo Barralier, Le Relais Occitan, 11800 Marseillette

Surrounded by vines, this fabulous old winery, with its giant oak vats, antique vineyard tools, and incredible glass-paved cellar, has been turned into a museum and four holiday cottages (two featured in this guide) by Anita and Jean-Louis. It's been a labour of love, but labours of love are nothing unusual for this energetic and cultured Franco-Italian couple. Both writers and journalists — their passions are history and poetry — you're as likely to discuss troubadour verse as 19th-century winemaking techniques over an impromptu aperitif in the vast barbecue area. The cottages, once the homes of the families working on the vineyard, have been refurbished with rustic simplicity. Furniture (mostly pine) and kitchen crockery are basic, with a Fifties feel. Lo Barralier, the oldest and smallest cottage, once inhabited by the barrel-maker, has a typical Languedocian staircase and a second-floor terrace with stunning views of the vineyards and the Montagne d'Alaric.

Sleeps: 2-5.
Price: €300-€365.
Bedrooms: 1 double with extra single bed on first floor; double sofabed on second floor; first floor shower & wc.

Booking details:
Jean Louis Cousin & Anita Canonica
Tel: +33 (0)4 68 79 12 67
Fax: +33 (0)4 68 79 12 67
E-mail: J-L.Cousin@wanadoo.fr
Web: www.perso.wanadoo.fr/relais.occitan

Map no: 18

Lo Podaire, Le Relais Occitan, 11800 Marseillette

Discuss troubadour music and history with your fellow residents over dinner above the old winery vaults; if you paint, Anita and Jean Louis might arrange an exhibition; or navigate the peaceful green waters of the Canal du Midi on Jean Louis' houseboat, hear him talk passionately about its history, and stop for local cheese, home-made preserves and some of the *domaine's* very drinkable wine. History and culture are what make the place and people tick here, so if topping up your tan by the pool or watching TV are what you're after, this is not for you — there are no pools or televisions here. Le Podaire, the vine-cutter's house, has a walnut staircase, wooden floors and knick-knacks brought back by Anita from travels in Africa and Asia. Enjoy views of the vineyards from the terrace of the tiny second-floor bedroom, and relax or dine on the bigger terrace in front. Further afield, there are Cathar castles to visit and hills to walk; the medieval fairytale city of Carcassonne, perched above the Aude, is a short drive away.

Sleeps: 4-7.
Price: €365-€460.
Bedrooms: 1 double with extra single bed; 1 childrens' twin; 1 double sofabed; bathroom; wc.

Booking details:
Jean Louis Cousin & Anita Canonica
Tel: +33 (0)4 68 79 12 67
Fax: +33 (0)4 68 79 12 67
E-mail: J-L.Cousin@wanadoo.fr
Web: www.perso.wanadoo.fr/relais.occitan

Mas Saint Jacques, 66300 Caixas

Welcome to the smallest village in France with a permanent population of one (plus a blind black cat who came with the house) and its own church and *Mairie*. In summer the population soars as Ian rents out two other houses but you'll still enjoy Caixas's remote mountain setting, stunning views down to the sea and fresh Catalan air. The 200-year-old farmhouse is simply but pleasingly furnished with country antiques. You have a large kitchen, a cosy dining room with working fireplace and a comfy living room with books, games and friendly armchairs, and a tiny patio in front for *al fresco* dining. Bedrooms are light and minimalist with polished wood floors and white walls and bedcovers. If you don't fancy the beach, climb the nearby Pic du Canigou (3,500m) and visit the still inhabited 11th-century monastery of Saint Martin along the way. Pop across the border to Spain and stock up on pots and paella, or laze by the walled pool and listen to the birdsong. *Due to circular staircase, unsuitable for young children or the infirm.*

Sleeps: 12.
Price: €1595-€2313 (£1,000-£1,450).
Bedrooms: 2 doubles, 1 twin, 1 room with bunkbed, all en suite; 1 suite: 1 double, 1 twin & bathroom.

Booking details:
Ian Mayes
Tel: +33 (0)4 68 38 87 83
Fax: +33 (0)4 68 38 87 83
E-mail: masstjacq@aol.com

  Map no: 18

Maison de la Place, 66300 Caixas

Once you would have heard the church bells toll from this restored Catalan stone cottage which is right on the Place de l'Église. Today the bells are silent and you can savour the deep peace and soul-soothing mountain views. Eat out in the sunken rose garden, just across the Place and watch the sun set, or relax here in the day with lizards and butterflies as your companions. Given the house's age, the interior is surprisingly modern, and the feel is light, clean and minimalist. The sitting/living room has cool tiled floors, a working fireplace and comfortable cream sofas, while the sweet kitchen has an older, more lived-in feel. Bedrooms have white walls with contrasting Persian rugs and one has a modern ironwork four-poster with delicate white drapes. Use the house as a base to walk the magical mountains or plunge into outdoor thermal baths. If you feel sociable, book yourself dinner at Ian's house where he runs a B&B: he's a talented cook and entertaining conversationalist. *Use of pool only outside high season.*

Sleeps: 5.
Price: €399-€638 (£250-£400).
Bedrooms: 2 doubles (1 with four-poster bed); 1 single; bathroom; wc.

Booking details:
Ian Mayes
Tel: +33 (0)4 68 38 87 83
Fax: +33 (0)4 68 38 87 83
E-mail: masstjacq@aol.com
Web: www.specialplacestostay.com

Garden House, 66300 Caixas

There are views even from the kitchen sink: mountains, including Pic du Canigou, tower above you; the Mediterranean glistens in the distance below and all around are fields and vineyards with a Corsican-style ruggedness. Although the Med is only 40 minutes away by car, the bustle of the coast seems hundreds of miles away. If nightlife is your thing, don't come here: cicadas, not discos, will sing you to sleep. Unlike the other two (rented) houses in this tiny hamlet, this white bungalow is new; it's attached to the main house but you have total privacy and peace with your own dreamy rose garden and terrace right in front. Inside is compact, airy and light, with cream walls and basic pine furniture. There's a white ironwork four-poster in the master bedroom and an extra single in the sitting room behind a screen. This is a great place to roam from: there are numerous nature reserves around the Massif of Canigou and if lucky you may spot Iberian lynx. If you fancy wine tasting, Ian the owner will direct you to some interesting new producers.

Sleeps: 2-3.
Price: €399-€598 (£250-£375).
Bedrooms: 1 four-poster double with bathroom & wc; single in sitting room; shower & wc.

Booking details:
Ian Mayes
Tel: +33 (0)4 68 38 87 83
Fax: +33 (0)4 68 38 87 83
E-mail: masstjacq@aol.com
Web: www.specialplacestostay.com

Map no: 18

Sardane, La Costa de Dalt, 66230 Prats de Mollo

Deeply peaceful, this 16th-century stone farmhouse high in the Pyrenees feels as if it's at the end of the earth. Join Gilbert tending his cattle and sheep in the forested hills, or watch Michelle making home-made sausage and pâtés (which you're welcome to buy). This dedicated and hardworking young couple will invite you to Sunday dinner: make sure you've worked up an appetite as Gilbert's cooking (Catalan and traditional French) is renowned, copious and unmissable. There are three cottages here, but 1.5 metre-thick walls ensure you'll rarely hear your neighbours. Interiors are cool and stylishly simple. Sardane has a vast monastic-style dining room with handmade wooden furniture, a terracotta tile floor and ancient roof beams. There's a huge stone fireplace, and attractive prints and photographs contrast with the whitewashed walls. You can tell you're near Spain by the rust-and-yellow handmade tiles in the immaculately equipped kitchen. Bedrooms have stupendous views, polished wooden floors — and, of course, huge old beams.

Sleeps: 6.
Price: €410-€490.
Bedrooms: 1 double with shower & wc; 1 double (2 extra single beds) with shower & wc.

Booking details:
Michelle & Gilbert Lanau
Tel: +33 (0)4 68 39 74 40
Fax: +33 (0)4 68 39 74 40
E-mail: ferme.auberge@free.fr

Map no: 18

173

Amérique du Sud, La Costa de Dalt, 66230 Prats de Mollo

Tranquil surroundings, mouth-watering interiors and Gilbert's gastronomic cooking mean you'll never want to leave this stone cottage hugging the Pyrenean hills. These magical mountains on the Spanish border are a treat for climbers and walkers. If you're less energetic, roam the Lanaus' 140 hectares, swim in the crystalline river, or pop down to the Med. The cottage is more modern in feel than the other two, but the old beams and terracotta tile floors are here, and the decoration is still pure, clutter-free and stylish. The entrance and most rooms are at first-floor level, apart from one bedroom downstairs, reached by an outdoor staircase. Beautiful handmade tiles and top-class equipment in the compact kitchen/dining room will inspire even lukewarm cooks (and you can impress your guests with the Lanaus' organic vegetables and home-made sausage and duck pâté). There's a fine stone fireplace to sit by if it's wet, and a terrace with unbeatable views for when it's fine. Blissful. *A third cottage, for five, can also be rented.*

Sleeps: 5.
Price: €410-€490.
Bedrooms: 2 doubles, each with extra single beds and own shower & wc.

Booking details:
Michelle & Gilbert Lanau
Tel: +33 (0)4 68 39 74 40
Fax: +33 (0)4 68 39 74 40
E-mail: ferme.auberge@free.fr

Rhône Valley – Alps

Photography by Michael Busselle.

Le Pigeonnier, Château du Bijou, 07210 Chomerac

The château, in whose grounds this quaintly-shaped stone building stands, was built by a local businessman for his little 'jewel' of a mistress. In World War Two it was the headquarters of the French Resistance until the Germans took it over — you can still see German graffiti on the walls. In one of the *pigeonnier*'s bedrooms the holes where pigeons flew in and out remain. Downstairs rooms (once storerooms and stables) have great vaulted stone ceilings. Old farm implements decorate the walls of the sitting room, but furniture and décor are modern, with plenty of pine, primrose-coloured walls, framed prints and white drapey curtains. French doors lead from the all-white sitting room to a small balustraded terrace and below there's another terrace and a private lawn with a view of the château. There's loads to do in the area, from canoeing in the gorges of the Ardèche, to horse-riding, to wine-tasting in local *caves*. *Pool is shared with two other houses, so there could be up to 14 others.*

Sleeps: 8-9.
Price: €1,435-€2,155 (£900-£1,350).
Bedrooms: 3 doubles, 1 with shower & wc; 1 twin; 1 single; shower & wc; bath & wc.

Booking details:
Mark & Jo Cutmore-Scott
Tel: +44 (0)1189 701901
Fax: +33 (0)1189 700192
E-mail: info@chateaudubijou.com
Web: www.chateaudubijou.com

La Petite Ferme, Château du Bijou, 07210 Chomerac

Space, homeliness and the delight of being in the grounds of a château are yours in this 300-year-old house. The hub is the big kitchen, where once the women made jam for the big house from apricots and pears grown in the orchards. You can see the vast wooden beams, the original bread oven (still charred) and the stone fireplace. One or two families could happily gather here to eat around the table or spill out onto the terrace and lawn, and there's a lovely lavender-fringed swimming pool beyond. Although there are two other cottages in the grounds (and you share the pool with their occupants), in your garden you have complete privacy. Furnishings are modern and low-budget, with plenty of paint-washed pine furniture, fitted carpets and brightly coloured walls. There's a large games room in the attic for rainy days. Otherwise, you can roam the wooded mountains all around, visit the Friday olive market at Nyons and the Thursday market in nearby Chomerac, or canoe in the Ardèche gorges. Do try the delicious local chestnuts.

Sleeps: 8.
Price: €1,435-€2,155 (£900-£1,350).
Bedrooms: 2 doubles, both with own bathroom & wc; 2 twins; shower & wc; sofabed downstairs.

Booking details:
Mark & Jo Cutmore-Scott
Tel: +44 (0)1189 701901
Fax: +44 (0)1189 700192
E-mail: info@chateaudubijou.com
Web: www.chateaudubijou.com

Académie, Le Fayet, 07110 Sanilhac

Stone dominates here: exposed stone walls and timeworn flagstone floors inside; outside, solid stone walls which tower above the chestnut forests for which the Ardèche is famous. Le Fayet is on the edge of a tiny farming hamlet, high in the hills, but the only traffic you're likely to hear is the daily postman's van. You can drink in the magnificent views from the terrace, prettily decorated with flower-filled terracotta pots. Cool off in the stone-vaulted dining/living room which still has the original three-tier stone washing basins, inglenook fireplace (which you can use) and bread oven and, of course, a deliciously uneven grey flagstone floor — a real piece of history. There's a light sitting room upstairs with terracotta tile floors, a mixture of modern cane and antique furniture, and stairs leading to a mezzanine floor with a double bed and a small roof terrace. Children will love the little terraced garden across the road, and there's a wide choice of rivers to bathe in or canoe on, including the famous Ardèche gorge, half an hour's drive away.

Sleeps: 6.
Price: €445-€520.
Bedrooms: 1 twin; 2 doubles, 1 on mezzanine; bathroom & wc; shower & wc.

Booking details:
Anna Niedeggen
Tel: +33 (0)4 75 39 93 75
Fax: +33 (0)4 75 39 92 79
E-mail: info@thebluehouse.net
Web: www.thebluehouse.net

Map no: 14

Estourel, Le Mas Bleu, 07260 Rosières

You might first spot your neighbours through the mists of the *hammam* (steam bath) or the bubbles of the jacuzzi, and they'll probably be German. Le Mas Bleu (The Blue House), with its seven blue-shuttered wisteria-clad apartments, may not be a typical Sawday choice, but it's certainly special. This 18th-century stone farmstead is superbly decorated, supremely peaceful (despite the presence of up to 30 other residents), and slightly alternative — some guests may bathe in the pool in the nude. It's run by an energetic and welcoming German couple: Anna, once a carpenter, and mother of two, and her partner Holger. They have restored the buildings with taste and sensitivity, keeping all the exteriors, and original beams, wherever possible. Estourel is the largest apartment, with two storeys and a large covered terrace with magnificent views of vineyards and mountains in almost every direction. The highlight inside is the vast antique dining table, once used to cut lengths of silk, for which the area is famous.

Sleeps: 6-7.
Price: €830-€992.
Bedrooms: 1 double; 2 doubles plus single; shower room & wc downstairs; shower room & wc upstairs.

Booking details:
Anna Niedeggen
Tel: +33 (0)4 75 39 93 75
Fax: +33 (0)4 75 39 92 79
E-mail: info@thebluehouse.net
Web: www.thebluehouse.net

Gounelle, Le Mas Bleu, 07260 Rosières

The views will inspire you: the blue mountains of Provence, Cévennes and the Massif Central are all visible, and all around are vines, more vines, and the sand-coloured houses of the hamlet of La Blacheyrette. If the inspiration moves you to create, there's an author's cafe in the grounds, where you can write (computer provided), make music, or dance. Or if the inspiration makes you feel sociable, there's a *hammam* (steam bath), a jacuzzi, and a games room with pool and table football and fridges stocked with local wines which you can drink on tab. Le Mas Bleu has seven apartments, of which Gounelle is the smallest, but you're assured privacy and peace here and have your own terrace and garden. The sitting/dining room has exposed stone walls, a mix of modern and antique pine furniture and a beautifully equipped kitchen area in one corner. The immaculate bedrooms are decorated with cheerful Provençal-style fabrics and have terracotta tile floors. This is a fabulous area for walking and cycling. Bikes are provided.

Sleeps: 2-5.
Price: €547-€685.
Bedrooms: 1 double; 1 double plus single; shower & wc.

Booking details:
Anna Niedeggen
Tel: +33 (0)4 75 39 93 75
Fax: +33 (0)4 75 39 92 79
E-mail: info@thebluehouse.net
Web: www.thebluehouse.net

Map no: 14

La Vieille Cure, 26340 Saint-Sauveur-en-Diois

The brass plaque of Christ on the door tells the house's history: this used to be the Priest's house, and it's bang in the heart of the ancient village just across the street from the church and the stone *lavoir*. No frills or overt luxury here and the restoration is rough-and-ready in places, but it will suit those seeking a taste of real French village life in a beautiful and remote mountain setting. Madame Dumond, who will probably greet you when you arrive, is a delight. Inside, the walls are traditional bare grey plaster, there's lots of pine and furnishings are simple. There's no garden, but the master bedroom leads to a covered terrace with table and chairs where you can eat out surrounded by stunning views of pine-clad mountains. Apart from the many long-distance footpaths, the valley is famous for its sparkling white wine, *Clairette de Die,* which locals claim predates champagne. You can buy it across the street from Adonis who also holds the key. *Fortnightly lets only.*

Sleeps: 5.
Price: €320-€445.
Bedrooms: 1 double; 1 large single; 1 twin; bathroom with bath & wc.

Booking details:
Lina Chivre-Dumond
Tel: +33 (0)4 75 59 71 70
Fax: +33 (0)4 75 59 75 24
E-mail: linadechivredumond@minitel.net

Map no: 14

180

La Roche Colombe, 26450 Charols

If you like the idea of socialising with other Anglophone families, you'll love it here. Bob and Celia Christmas also run a B&B, and in the evenings everyone dines out in the huge arched courtyard under the plane trees. Bob, who used to be an interior designer and architect, and his wife, Celia, ex-rag trade, are an entertaining and sociable couple who have restored this 200-year-old stone farmhouse and outbuildings over the years. The swish self-catering apartment, L'Hermitage, includes a bedroom with a four-poster bed, pale and pretty with pure white drapes, and a large living room with kilims and a big fireplace. The children's room is furnished in more functional pine and primary colours. If you prefer to eat *en famille* you can sit on the balcony overhanging the courtyard and revel in views of the pretty medieval village of Manas and the Drôme mountains. There's a swimming pool, hidden behind the house, which is shared with B&B guests. *Meals on request.*

Sleeps: 4
Price: €640-€896.
Bedrooms: 1 double; 1 childrens' twin; bathroom with bath, shower & wc.

Booking details:
Bob & Celia Christmas
Tel: +33 (0)4 75 90 48 22
E-mail: rochecolombe@hotmail.com
Web: www.bbfrance.com/xmas.html

Map no: 14

Salivet, 26460 Truinas

Few places have it all, but this must be one. Breathtaking mountain views, a lovely owner and a fascinating building combine to make this a truly special place. The honey-stone house stands where the oxen sheds and haylofts used to be; the ruins of the original farmhouse are still visible in the garden. Jane, an English artist who specialises in silk screen printing, and her German architect partner have restored and furnished the place simply but beautifully with old beams, terracotta tile floors, whitewashed walls, stone fireplaces and antique furniture. On summer nights you can sleep on the roof terrace. During the day, sit on the terrace under the wisteria, snooze on the lawn under the weeping willow or cool off in the (shared) pool. Jane sells honey, home-made jams and truffles in season, and if you fancy wine-tasting there are excellent vineyards half an hour away. Jane rents out another house next door and lives close by. *Closed November-April. Meals on request.*

Sleeps: 6 + 1 baby.
Price: €638-€1,244 (£400-780).
Bedrooms: 2 singles; 1 double;
1 double with cot; 2 wcs; shower;
bathroom & wc.

Booking details:
Jane Worthington
Tel: +33 (0)4 75 53 49 13
Fax: +33 (0)4 75 53 37 31

Rossignol, 26460 Truinas

You'll hear nightingales here in May, as the name suggests. At the end of a small track among the high mountains of the Drôme, nature-lovers and walkers will love this old rose-strewn stone house – the photo does not do it justice. Jane, the artist owner who lives next door, will supply walking itineraries, maps and flower guides. Look out for Venus Slippers, Pasque flowers and Lizard orchids. An inspired cook, too, Jane will provide dinner if you ask in advance. She makes a terrific pâté from organic pork from the farm down the road. Inside, the highlight is the vast carpeted double bedroom with huge dark beams, stone fireplace, piano and oak four-poster bed. The terracotta-floored kitchen has an original stone sink; in the bathroom next door the bath surround is made from church pews and Tunisian ceramic tiles. There is another larger house next door, so this would be ideal for families holidaying together. *Closed November-April.*

Sleeps: 4-6.
Price: €511-€798 (£320-£500).
Bedrooms: 1 four-poster with 2 single sofabeds; 1 twin with wc; bathroom & wc.

Booking details:
Jane Worthington
Tel: +33 (0)4 75 53 49 13
Fax: +33 (0)4 75 53 37 31

  Map no: 14

Domaine de Saint-Luc, 26790 La Baume de Transit

Wine, truffles, tranquillity: here you have great ingredients for a delicious holiday. The wine is produced by your hosts, Ludovic and Eliane, from the vineyards all around the *domaine*: they'll be happy to sell you their prized Cotes-du-Rhône Villages or invite you to a *dégustation*. The holm oaks behind your house are where the truffles grow, and during the winter Ludovic runs truffle weekends which culminate in a dinner with every course containing the local delicacy. Furnishings in this pretty, split-level studio, ideal for a couple with a child, are minimalist but stylish, with delicate ironwork tables and chairs, terracotta tile floors and bright ceramic tiles in the kitchen and shower. On lazy summer days relax among the olive trees and lavender by the huge pool, read on your private terrace to the song of cicadas, or visit the numerous markets in the towns around. You can occasionally join the Cornillon's B&B guests for dinner in the main house across the courtyard — ask in advance. *Another self-catering studio to rent next door.*

Sleeps: 2-3.
Price: €565-€690.
Bedrooms: 1 double on mezzanine level; 1 single in open-plan living room; shower & wc.

Booking details:
Ludovic & Eliane Cornillon
Tel: +33 (0)4 75 98 11 51
Fax: +33 (0)4 75 98 19 22
Web: www.dom-saint-luc.com

Map no: 14

L'Amiradou, 26170 Mérindol-les-Oliviers

The name means 'place with a view' and you won't be disappointed: the white granite flank of Mont Ventoux is in the distance, and all around, herb-scented hills, vineyards and olive groves. In fact the builder who helped Susan and Andrew do up this farm labourer's cottage thought they'd made a mistake as the rented house has better views than theirs below. Your hosts, who used to work for Marks & Spencer in Paris, will be happy to advise you on local trips, but will be otherwise discreet, and the pool, barbecue and garden (where the very best views are) are totally yours. The house is immaculate, light and attractively furnished with antique pine, lots of it, like the lovely pine sink surround in one bathroom, brought from England. A vast granite-topped pine baker's table separates the kitchen from the sitting/dining room. You'll spend most of your time, though, on the terrace among the lavender and honeysuckle, by the pool, or visiting nearby Vaison-la-Romaine. The owners claim the bakery down the road (also a restaurant) makes the best bread in Provence.

Sleeps: 4.
Price: €479-€957 (£300-£600).
Bedrooms: 1 double with own separate bathroom & wc; 1 twin with bathroom & wc.

Booking details:
Susan Smith
Tel: +33 (0)4 75 28 78 69
Fax: +33 (0)4 75 28 78 69
E-mail: smitha@club-internet.fr
Web: www.lamiradou.com

Map no: 14

Maison des Gardes, Rue du Centre, 26400 Allex

Since the 11th century the stone houses of Allex, like those in the other *villages perchés* in this region, have huddled together high on a hill around a castle to keep enemies at bay. This remarkable house, built in the 16th century, was where the castle guards lived. The front walls were the defensive walls of the village and there was even a secret passage to the château. Built on three levels, linked by a staircase in the turret, it's deceptively large. Parisian owner Sophie's passion is collecting pottery cicadas, and you'll find them in all shapes and sizes throughout the house. Beautiful antique furniture, plush white sofas and a large stone fireplace give the vast and light sitting room an aristocratic air. Décor in the master bedroom is more experimental, with yellow rag-rolled walls and matching bedspread, and cicada stencilling on the walls. French windows lead out to a large roof terrace. This is the perfect house to experience the life of a lively, authentic French village in a beautiful corner of France. Writers will love it.

Sleeps: 8.
Price: €600-€735.
Bedrooms: 2 doubles, 1 with own bathroom & wc; 2 twins; shared bathroom & wc; wc.

Booking details:
Sophie Le Norcy
Tel: +33 (0)1 45 78 99 61
Fax: +33 (0)1 42 24 40 68
E-mail: le-norcy.s@wanadoo.fr

Map no: 14

Les Granges, 73700 Bourg-Saint-Maurice

Come here in summer and walk in flower-filled Alpine pastures to the tinkle of cowbells; stay in winter and ski, virtually from the front door, on some of France's finest slopes. In a pretty mountain hamlet on the edge of the Vanoise National Park, this chalet is cool in summer, cosy in winter, and always welcoming. Once the barn to the farmhouse next door, it has been skilfully converted to ensure its balconies (choose which one suits your mood) are not overlooked; its one-metre-thick outside walls ensure peace and quiet. The inside has been newly decorated with high-quality pine-panelled walls and floors, and pine furniture. After an active day out, relax by the open fire in the beautiful modern sitting room with its high-backed pine settle, baby blue and white striped cushions, and clean cream walls. If you're here to ski, jump on the funicular just 100 metres down the lane to Les Arcs. In summer, walk in the mountains (look out for Alpine ibex), or pop into Bourg-St-Maurice for a taste of Savoyard cuisine.

Sleeps: 6-8.
Price: €638-€1,516 (Feb) (£400-£950).
Bedrooms: 2 doubles; 2 twins; bathroom; shower; 2 wcs.

Booking details:
Yda & Rupert Morgan
Tel: +44 (0)1576 300 232
Fax: +44 (0)1576 300 818
E-mail: morganbellows@yahoo.co.uk
will change soon info@morganbellows.co.uk

Map no: 15

Chalet Chatillon, 74450 Le Grand Bornand

Smell the wood, listen to the silence and drink in the marvellous mountain views. In winter, take the ski lift at the end of the road to the pleasant resort of Chinaillon and in summer, laze in the Alpine meadows to the tinkle of cowbells. This architect-designed, traditional-style wooden chalet is one of three owned by André and Stéphane, a young, hardworking French couple who will go to extraordinary lengths to ensure you enjoy your stay. They live next door and they'll bring breakfast to your large dining table if you want to be totally spoiled; they'll even teach you to ski, too. Inside, high-quality pine ceilings and walls contrast with grey tiled floors and the occasional grey exposed stone wall, creating an atmosphere of comfort and cosiness. Furniture is functional and new and there's a woodburner to relax by after a long day in the mountains skiing. Cocoon yourself in sweet-smelling pine in the simple but pretty bedrooms with excellent linen and views. Shops, restaurants and cross-country skiing are all close by. A gem.

Sleeps: 11.
Price: €700-€2,820 (Feb).
Bedrooms: 2 twins, 1 with shower & wc; 2 doubles; 1 triple; bathroom; wc; shower & wc.

Booking details:
André & Stéphane Deloche
Tel: +33 (0)4 50 27 01 65
Fax: +33 (0)4 50 27 01 65
E-mail: stephane.deloche@wanadoo.fr

Provence – Alps – Riviera

Photography by Michael Busselle.

La Maison de Brian, 04150 Simiane la Rotonde

This 16th-century house is named after a writer friend of Martine's, and Martine herself is an artist and runs the pottery next door. Whether you're artistic or not, there's plenty to inspire you in Simiane, perched majestically on a rocky outcrop with views of the lavender fields below. Medieval paved alleys wind between aristocratic stone houses with heavy carved doors, and the stunning covered hall of the old market is just two minutes' walk away. Tall and thin like its neighbours, the Maison de Brian used to be the cobbler's and the original benches were still here when Martine restored it. The house has now been thoroughly modernised and furniture is basic but adequate with plentiful use of pine panelling on walls and ceilings. There's a wonderful large sitting/dining room with solid antique furniture, heavy beams, exposed stone walls and copious books. The house can sleep four or seven, depending on whether you rent all three storeys or just the lower storey. Enjoy this magical place from your own tiny terrace behind the house.

Sleeps: 4 (or 7).
Price: €185-€425 for 4 (€275-€595 for 7).
Bedrooms: 1 double with bathroom & wc; sofabed; wc. (1 double; 1 single on mezzanine; shower & wc.)

Booking details:
Martine Cazin
Tel: +33 (0)4 92 75 90 60
Fax: +33 (0)4 92 75 90 60

Mas des Genets, Quartier St-Donat, 84400 Saignon

Set among vineyards and lavender fields just below the pretty village of Saignon, which perches like a fort on turrets of white rock, this one-up-one-down stone cottage is a peaceful retreat in the popular Luberon. Reached by a private drive, it's part of a farmhouse which has been skilfully converted by American-born Stephen and his English wife Meg, who live in the main part of the house. There's another apartment for two next door, but each property has its own private terrace and lawn where you'll enjoy birdsong and mountain views. This corner house used to be the tractor shed; upstairs were the storerooms. There are original beams, new terracotta tiles, and modern pine tables and chairs. There's a functional kitchenette in one corner, and upstairs, a small bedroom with a brass bed, sloping beamed ceilings and blue and green floral blinds. Take the footpath to Saignon or walk in the Luberon hills. And don't miss the superb Saturday market in Apt.

Sleeps: 2.
Price: €305-€535.
Bedrooms: 1 double; shower & wc.

Booking details:
Meg & Stephen Parker
Tel: +33 (0)4 90 04 65 33
Fax: +33 (0)4 90 74 56 85
E-mail: masdegenet@aol.com

Map no: 14

Place de la Fontaine, 84400 Saignon

Listen to the bubbling village fountain and the soothing murmur of the voices of outdoor diners from the pristine comfort of your white-linened bed. You're in the central square of this stunning, but lesser known, Luberon village and you'll enjoy it from a home that is both stylish and luxurious. Henrietta, its Australian owner, has decorated the ancient three-storey stone house with artistic flair, while skilfully respecting its character. Soothing and sophisticated ochres and creams in the kitchen and living room are enhanced by attractive *objets d'art*, like pottery jugs and antique taps which Henrietta has picked up from local *brocantes* or craftsmen. Kitchen floors and work surfaces have attractive old wood borders, and immaculate crockery is stored on free-standing ironwork shelves. Light, minimalist bedrooms have original wooden doors and beams, basketwork tables and simple concrete floors. The airy double on the third floor has a tiny flower-decked terrace that gives onto the beauty of Provence.

Sleeps: 6-8.
Price: €700-€1,000.
Bedrooms: 2 doubles, 1 with own shower & wc; 1 twin; bathroom & wc; 2 double sofabeds in living room.

Booking details:
Henrietta Taylor
Tel: +33 (0)4 90 75 49 64
Fax: +33 (0)4 90 75 49 37
E-mail: vacances@bigpond.com

Map no: 14

Rose Cottage, Rue Celey, 84400 Saignon

The heart of Saignon, perched precariously along a vast saddle of rock, is only a minute's walk away, but here you look onto a sleepy, stone-paved square where cats roam, geraniums bloom and tranquillity is yours. Inside, Australian owner Henrietta, who lives in a nearby village, has created a refreshing mood of light and space through a stylish blend of pure white walls and natural honey-coloured stone. Even the kitchen sink and work surfaces are made of the soothing stone, and no expense has been spared in bringing original features back to life. Old doors have been superbly restored, the age-worn stone stairs have been kept and a stunning stone vaulted *cave* serves as a utility room. Furniture is minimalist, much of it ironwork, and Henrietta has added stylish touches like twigwork animals and handcrafted curtain rods. Bedrooms, with deliciously luxurious linen, are light and white, and showers, with Salernes tiles, provide the odd splash of colour. Luberon without the crowds. Perfect.

Sleeps: 4.
Price: €615-€920.
Bedrooms: 1 twin with shower & wc;
1 double with shower & wc.

Booking details:
Henrietta Taylor
Tel: +33 (0)4 90 75 49 64
Fax: +33 (0)4 90 75 49 37
E-mail: vacances@bigpond.com

Map no: 14

L'Oustaou, 84410 Crillon le Brave

Hélène, the dynamic, elegant owner who lives next door, has put her natural artistic flair to good use in this tiny cottage on the site of the old farm barn. Colourful and stylish with high-quality furnishings, it's a lovely place for two. Keep yourselves to yourselves on your sun-drenched terrace (there's a hammock from which to gaze at the mountain views); or socialise with the occupants of the other small cottage on the other side of the large farmhouse, and enjoy the gentle goings-on on this Provençal smallholding. Whatever your choice, there's plenty of space in the one-hectare garden whose lawns and orchards sweep down to a shared swimming pool and a bubbling stream. Hélène will ply you with eggs from her chickens and geese, fresh apricots and home-made jams. If you're lucky you may get to taste her apricot tart, and she'll cook you dinner if you ask in advance. Stroll into the historic village, just up the road, for shops and restaurants; explore the area by foot or bicycle (borrow bikes here); or indulge in a little *dégustation* at one of the many vineyards.

Sleeps: 2.
Price: €426-€732.
Bedrooms: 1 twin/double; shower & wc.

Booking details:
Bridget Whitehead
Tel: +33 (0)4 90 61 71 22
Fax: +33 (0)4 90 61 71 22
E-mail: robin.bridget@wanadoo.fr

Domaine la Condamine, 84410 Crillon le Brave

Seven generations of wine-growers have breathed their first in this pretty 17th-century *domaine*, and Madame, an energetic businesswoman, organises tastings of her own *Coteaux du Ventoux*. The apartment, at the far end of the farmstead, has its own private entrance and a courtyard where you can dine on sultry evenings. Colours in the large, well-equipped kitchen and sitting room downstairs are soft and southern: terracottas, mellow golds and creams. The three bedrooms upstairs have stylish painted furniture, hand-painted decorative wall borders and magnificent views across the vineyards to Mont Ventoux. You'll have company around the pool as Madame also runs a large B&B. Guests dine on the terrace of the main house. There's plenty to do if you want to get out and about: visit the lively Monday market in nearby Bédoin or the larger one in Vaison-la-Romaine on Tuesdays, stock up on wine at the local *caves*, or discover the area by bike or foot.

Sleeps: 6.
Price: €760-€915.
Bedrooms: 1 double; 2 twins; bathroom; wc.

Booking details:
Marie-José Eydoux
Tel: +33 (0)4 90 62 47 28
Fax: +33 (0)4 90 62 47 28
E-mail: domlacondamine@hotmail.com
Web: domainelacondamine.here.de

Map no: 14

Le Mas des Maridats, 84410 Bedoin

Sophistication, simplicity and solidity characterise this three-storey *maison de maître* on the edge of the hamlet of Les Maridats. The Dutch owners are passionate about interior design and antiques, and the house could well feature in the magazines on the coffee tables. Colours are bold — there's an olive green ceiling in the dining area and yellow walls in one bedroom — and they work. Ancient clay pots, wicker baskets and old prints are stylishly arranged and the owners have taken care to keep original features like old stone fireplaces and the timeworn terracotta tiles and wooden edgings on the stairs. The kitchen door at the back leads to a vast covered terrace and a small, unfenced swimming pool among rosemary and lavender bushes; views to the vineyards are all around and the jagged peaks of the Dentelles de Montmirail are in the distance. Although the house stands on the corner of two quiet roads, the garden and terrace are perfectly private. From here you can visit gems like Vaison-la-Romaine, Avignon and Gordes.

Sleeps: 7 + 1 baby.
Price: €660-€2,000.
Bedrooms: 1 double with shower & wc; 1 double with cot; 1 single; 1 twin; bathroom; wc; cloakroom with wc & basin downstairs.

Booking details:
Bridget Whitehead
Tel: +33 (0)4 90 61 71 22
Fax: +33 (0)4 90 61 71 22
E-mail: robin.bridget@wanadoo.fr

Map no: 14

Les Vignes, 84410 Flassan

The old oxcarts are still in the outhouses: for centuries this isolated cluster of buildings at the foot of the mighty Mont Ventoux was a farm. It's recently been restored by the French owner, who lives in the nearby village of Flassan and is on hand if you need anything or want to practice your French. This is serious wine country and all around are rolling vine-clad hills and *caves* where you can taste and buy wine. Inside the feel is definitely new although the owner has taken care to use Provençal-style terracotta tile floors, cheerful blue and yellow fabrics and paint-washed pine furniture. The bedrooms have vast exposed beams and stone walls, sloping ceilings and magnificent views. Ceramic pots with dried lavender and grasses, tiny wall alcoves and brass-rimmed porthole windows provide touches of originality. At the end of a long track, with no houses nearby, there's total peace and privacy. If you're feeling active, there's Mont Ventoux to climb and the towns of Avignon and Vaison-la-Romaine to visit.

Sleeps: 6-7.
Price: €560-€1,860.
Bedrooms: 3 doubles, 1 with extra single bed; bathroom with bath & wc.

Booking details:
Bridget Whitehead
Tel: +33 (0)4 90 61 71 22
Fax: +33 (0)4 90 61 71 22
E-mail: robin.bridget@wanadoo.fr

Map no: 14

Chambre de Séjour avec Vue, 84400 Saignon

Walk through the door and you could be in a Dali painting: neon lights sprout, phallus-like, from chairs; torn strips of calico hang like skeletons from hangers on the landing. You may have to blink to believe it's all real. This minimalist, fantastical world, contained within the ancient walls of a three-storey Provençal village house, is the creation of Kamila and Pierre, a Polish-Franco couple who run their house as a contemporary arts centre. Talk art over an exquisite home-cooked dinner in the stylish dining room with B&B guests and resident artists — and sip your coffee beside displays of their work in the sitting room-gallery next door. If you want privacy, cook amid the whiter-than-white splendour of your apartment at the back of the house. Admire the multi-coloured designer-made wooden sofa, and wash away the rigours of the day in the blue bathroom, with its late 19th-century olive enamel bath, original oil painting and antique English basin. *An apartment for three is also available.*

Sleeps: 2.
Price: €457.
Bedrooms: 1 double; bathroom & wc.

Booking details:
Kamila Regent & Pierre Jaccaud
Tel: +33 (0)4 90 04 85 01
Fax: +33 (0)4 90 04 85 01
E-mail: chambreavecvue@vox-pop.net
Web: www.chambreavecvue.com

Map no: 14

Jas des Eydins, 84480 Bonnieux

In open countryside with views of the Luberon hills all around, and reached by a dirt track, this is a place where you can completely unwind. Sit in the large garden, enveloped by the scent of roses and lavender, and learn the meaning of bliss. The 18th-century stone buildings, once a sheepfold and part of a Provençal farm, were restored by their architect owner, Jan, and his elegant art historian wife, Shirley, who live next door. The style is luxurious and there's a successful mix of country antiques and modern furniture in the large kitchen and sitting room, and in the three bedrooms, which are in a separate building. Snuggle up on cooler evenings by the log fire. On hot summer days wallow in the pool and revel in beautiful views of Mont Ventoux; in the evenings dine out on the large terrace to the song of the cicadas. Shirley and Jan are on hand if you need them, but will also leave you to have a relaxing holiday in privacy. *Fourth twin bedroom available in main house, with independent entrance, at extra cost.*

Sleeps: 6.
Price: €1,250-€1,850.
Bedrooms: 2 twin/doubles each with own bathroom & wc; twin with shower & wc.

Booking details:
Shirley & Jan Kozlowski
Tel: +33 (0)4 90 75 84 99
Fax: +33 (0)4 90 75 96 71
E-mail: eydins@pacwan.fr

Map no: 14

La Maison Bleue, Hameau de Garandeau, 13410 Lambesc

Owner Christine de Labouchère's passions are old stone, paint, and tomatoes, and if they're yours too, you'll love it here. The house is part of a 17th-century hamlet where, in turn, coypus (for furs), silkworms and pigs have been reared. Christine, an interior designer, has converted the old stone buildings with astounding results. Walls and furniture alike have a sophisticated distressed look, achieved by adding egg to the paint, and applying it with a rag: if you're interested, Christine will share her paint recipes. The Maison Bleue is perhaps the most perfect of the three, very different, self-catering houses here: the Provençal blue shutters, vines over the door and tiny terrace make it look almost like a dolls' house. Inside, all is blue, from the two bedrooms and bathrooms to the crockery. The atmosphere is one of stylish luxury. And the tomatoes... Christine also grows old varieties of tomatoes, and in season will probably leave a basketful at your door. *Breakfast available in main house, €8 p.p.*

Sleeps: 4.
Price: €1,067-€1,525.
Bedrooms: 2 doubles each with own shower; separate wc.

Booking details:
Christine de Labouchère
Tel: +33 (0)4 42 57 26 31
Fax: +33 (0)4 42 57 25 96
E-mail: infos@3vallons.com
Web: www.3vallons.com

Le Pigeonnier, Hameau de Garandeau, 13410 Lambesc

You can still see the holes in the wall where pigeons flew in and out when this tiny 17th-century hamlet was last inhabited. Owner Christine, who lives in the large house around the corner, has really gone to town with the paint here, matching as far as possible the original colours. She's even left a patch of wall untouched so you can see the layers of different paints over the years. Downstairs rooms are decorated in rusts and oranges, matching the Twenties floor tiles. But the highlight is the *chambre haute*, in sumptuous cream, and its outrageous scarlet-washed shower room with a pebble and decking floor. Despite its sophistication, the house feels like a home with books everywhere, and Christine will make sure the flowers are kept fresh throughout your stay. None of the houses here are overlooked, so on languid summer days you can lounge in privacy on the terrace and pluck grapes from the vine over the door. Roam the 51-hectare estate, and visit the treasures of Aix, Avignon and Arles.

Sleeps: 6.
Price: €1,525-€2,287.
Bedrooms: 3 doubles, each with shower and wc.

Booking details:
Christine de Labouchère
Tel: +33 (0)4 42 57 26 31
Fax: +33 (0)4 42 57 25 96
E-mail: infos@3vallons.com
Web: www.3vallons.com

Map no: 14

Le Bastidon, Hameau de Garandeau, 13410 Lambesc

All is light, space and simplicity in this former resin store hidden in the pine trees. The building may be three centuries old but it's been thoroughly modernised: the only reminders of the past are the roof beams and wooden artefacts from Bali and Indonesia, collected by owner Christine on her travels. These contrast well with the cream fabrics and paintwork of the communal rooms. Colour schemes in the bedrooms aim to shock: raspberry walls and orange bedcovers in the downstairs twin; yellow ochre in the upstairs double, with a grey and natural stone bathroom. Sliding doors lead you onto the huge terrace where you could spend hours listening to the cicadas and breathing in the scent of the pine trees and wild herbs. There's a boules pitch, and the pool is just a few metres away (in the day you'll be sharing it with three other houses in the hamlet). If you don't feel like cooking, Christine will order ready-cooked meals from the delicatessen, and you can eat breakfast at the main house if you wish.

Sleeps: 4.
Price: €1,677-€2,440.
Bedrooms: 1 twin; bathroom and wc;
1 double with shower room; wc.

Booking details:
Christine de Labouchère
Tel: +33 (0)4 42 57 26 31
Fax: +33 (0)4 42 57 25 96
E-mail: infos@3vallons.com
Web: www.3vallons.com

Map no: 14

La Maison Blanche, 83830 Bargemon

You're outside one of the prettiest and most fashionable villages of East Provence but here, incredibly, you see and are seen by nobody. Cradled by an amphitheatre of pine-clad mountains, this old farmhouse is surrounded by lawns, flower-filled meadows and orchards. In spring you'll hear nightingales and smell wild narcissi and in summer the fruit trees yield a feast of apricots, cherries and figs (all of which you're free to pick). On lazy summer days eat on the huge terrace under the shade of the lime trees. The house has been completely renovated by the English owners, although they have kept old beams and some red hexagonal floor tiles. Furniture is mostly antique French and English, with some unusual items, like an ancient workbench-turned-sideboard in the dining room, and wooden doughboards at the heads of two of the beds. The lovely end bedroom, once the hayloft, has a vine-clad balcony from which you can pluck grapes in the autumn. As bedrooms are reached by two staircases, the house is ideal for two families holidaying together.

Sleeps: 10.
Price: €750-€3,111 (£470-£1,950).
Bedrooms: 4 twins, 1 with shower & wc, 2 with bath & wc; 1 double; shared bathroom & wc.

Booking details:
Janet Hill
Tel: +44 (0)1628 482579
Fax: +44 (0)1628 482579
E-mail: dsimons@onetel.net.uk

      Map no: 15

Les Pêchers, 83400 Isle de Porquerolles

Wonderful Porquerolles! An off-season island retreat for a select few — and for masses more in high summer. The pretty village and harbour, where the ferry docks, are the nerve centre of island life. Cars are forbidden so hire your bikes here to explore the pure white sandy beaches and cliffs, the vineyards and pheasant-thronged woods; or sit and sponge up the atmosphere wafting from the restaurants and shops gathered round the large boules square. Les Pêchers, built in the '60s on the road to the lighthouse by the family who used to own the island, stands in a big, nostalgically crumbly garden with vines and a peach tree, and a large inviting patio-terrace where life is mostly lived under the fading bamboo awning. The interior is pure '60s. Floors are porridge tiles, walls are strong-coloured paint, the one bathroom is so old-fashioned as to have become fashionable again: just a high, deep bath, retro basin and bidet; bedrooms are comfortably furnished with bourgeois chests of drawers and big *armoires* guarding good blankets; the well-fitted kitchen is light and just as comfortingly 'family'. A super place for a family holiday.

Sleeps: 6-8.
Price: €1,000-€1,900.
Bedrooms: 2 doubles; 1 twin with extra bed; bathroom; wc.

Booking details:
Christine Richet
Tel: (0)6 07 10 06 35
Fax: (0)4 94 58 35 43
E-mail: richet@cnam.fr

Hameau l'Autourière, 83680 La Garde Freinet

The tortuous drive along a track to this ancient hamlet is worth the bumps. Climb the eight stone steps to your single-floor cottage and you reach a haven of rustic cosiness. Warm rusts, creams and yellows enhance the feeling of comfort, as do the attractive ethnic artefacts brought back from Africa where Mrs Woodall, the English owner, used to farm before she made Provence her home. Ancient terracotta tiled floors, tiny windows and low beamed ceilings convey the great age of this stone *magnanerie* where silkworms used to be reared for the farmhouses next door. Mrs Woodall lives in one of them with Cleo, her golden Labrador, and often hosts a stream of friends, grandchildren and B&B guests. You may meet them in the magnificent pool among the trees, but if you want privacy there is plenty of space among the three-odd hectares of meadows, lawns and borders, skilfully tended by Mrs Woodall's green fingers. Visit medieval and fashionable La Garde Freinet, and walk the GR9 (*Route des Crêtes*) through the rugged Massif des Maures.

Sleeps: 2-4.
Price: €399-€638 (£250-£400).
Bedrooms: 1 double plus 2 single campbeds for children; bathroom & wc.

Booking details:
Mrs Philippa Woodall
Tel: +33 (0)4 94 43 63 47

Map no: 15

La Vieille Ferme, Pimaquet, 83570 Entrecasteaux

The perfect place to laze on languid summer days: here are flower-filled meadows, vine-draped terraces and a lawn hidden among the cypresses. And if you suddenly feel energetic, there are woods and hills to explore, and a cool river in which to bathe or fish for trout. The most remarkable feature, though, is a Roman irrigation canal behind the house, fast-flowing and pristine, for which Mimi, the owner, pays £10 a year for the privilege of using. The stone farmhouse is more modern — a mere 300 years old. The donkey once lived where the sitting room is and the old wooden manger is still in one corner. Furnishings are homely and well-used rather than lavish. There's a large double bedroom with solid antiques upstairs, while bathrooms are colourfully decorated with handmade tiles from nearby Salernes. Mimi, a painter and ex-university lecturer, lives in the lovely house next door, or in a caravan when the house is rented. Be sure to visit the 12th-century Cistercian Thoronet Abbey nearby. *Swimming pool planned.*

Sleeps: 6-8 + 1 baby.
Price: €877 (£550).
Bedrooms: 2 doubles, both with extra single bed, 1 with own bathroom & wc; 1 twin; shower & wc.

Booking details:
Mrs June Watkins
Tel: +44 (0)208 891 2656
E-mail: junewatkins@lineone.net

Map no: 14

Les Palmiers, 06400 Cannes

Don't be deceived by the banal-looking exterior of the Seventies' block in which this exquisite studio apartment stands. This is a real jewel. From your bed you can watch the glistening waters of the Bay of Cannes and listen to the palm trees gently rustling in the breeze. And all around are beautiful furnishings and antiques selected by the owner (who lives next door with her Scots terrier, Little Boy). Full of grace and tremendous kindness, Edith used to be a fashion model, which goes some way towards explaining her flair and attention to detail: fruit bowls and fresh flowers are painstakingly arranged to ensure you feel pampered. There was even a plate of melon and Parma ham in the fridge when I arrived. There are basic cooking facilities in the passage between the living room and the bathroom, and you can eat outside on the tiny garden terrace. The beach and local markets are both 10 minutes by bus and Edith will update you on exhibitions. *Minimum stay three nights.*

Sleeps: 2.
Price: €80-€125 per night.
Bedrooms: 1 twin/double; bathroom & wc.

Booking details:
Edith Lefay
Tel: +33 (0)4 93 69 25 67

Map no: 15

La Bergerie, 06620 Le Bar sur Loup

The old stone walls of the *bergerie* (which means shepherd's hut) will keep you cool in the hottest weather. Enjoy your morning croissants inside, where the original manger has been turned into a breakfast bar, or on the terrace, watching the sun come up over the pretty village of Le Bar sur Loup across the valley. Surrounded by olive groves, pine trees and rocky-peaked mountains, here is total peace. Sylvie, an actress, and her biologist husband Pascal, have restored and decorated the house in a stylish but simple, relaxed way. Floors and ceilings are in painted wood; the bedroom has fabulous views in every direction. The charming young couple and their two little boys will make you feel at home, yet leave you to your own devices. From here you are only a short hop from the coast if you fancy the razzmatazz of the Riviera, or explore the stunning 'perched villages' of the area. There is another more modern, slightly larger cottage to rent, 50 metres away, which sleeps two, plus child.

Sleeps: 2-3.
Price: €350-€520.
Bedrooms: 1 double; sofabed
downstairs; shower; wc.

Booking details:
Sylvie & Pascal Delaunay
Tel: +33 (0)4 93 42 50 08
Fax: +33 (0)4 93 42 50 08

Map no: 15

Quick Reference Indices

Quick Reference Indices

Quick Reference Indices

Quick Reference Indices

WALKING

Exceptional walks nearby. Very many other rural properties are also surrounded by good walking country.

Quick Reference Indices

Quick Reference Indices

PUBLIC TRANSPORT

These owners have told us that their self-catering property can be reached by public transport.

Picardy
5 • 8

Alsace
11

Normandy
35

Western Loire
45 • 46 • 48

Loire Valley
50 • 53 • 55 • 56

Poitou - Charentes
60 • 63

Aquitaine
84 • 97 • 98

Midi - Pyrénées
101 • 119

Languedoc - Roussillon
147 • 150 • 151 • 155 • 163

Rhône Valley - Alps
178 • 179 • 186 • 188

Provence - Alps - Riviera
194 • 206

NO CAR?

These owners have told us that they are happy to collect you from the nearest bus or train station - please check when booking.

The North
1

Picardy
5 • 8

Burgundy
17

Normandy
28 • 35 • 37

Brittany
39

Western Loire
41 • 42 • 45 • 46

Loire Valley
50 • 51 • 52 • 56

Poitou - Charentes
59 • 61 • 62 • 65 • 66 • 68

Limousin
69 • 72

Aquitaine
74 • 77 • 83 • 84 • 85 • 87 • 88 • 89 • 93 • 97

Midi - Pyrénées
101 • 105 • 107 • 108 •110 • 111 • 113 • 120 • 123 • 124 • 125 • 129

Auvergne
140

Languedoc - Roussillon
147 • 150 • 151 • 155 • 163 • 166 • 168 • 169

Rhône Valley - Alps
175 • 177 • 178 • 179 • 182 • 186 • 188

Provence - Alps - Riviera
197 • 203 • 206

French words and expressions

Chambre d'Hôtes - B&B

Table d'hôtes - dinner with the owners of the house

Gîte - self-catering holiday house, usually attached to owner's house or a farm (see Introduction)

Gîte d'Étape - overnight dormitory-style huts/houses, often run by the local village or municipality, for cyclists or walkers (often with optional meals)

Gîte Panda - may be either a *Chambre d'Hôtes* or a self-catering house in a national or regional park; owners provide information about flora and fauna, walking itineraries, sometimes guided walks and will lend binoculars, even rucksacks

Château - a mansion or stately home built for aristocrats between the 16th and 19th centuries. A 'castle', with fortifications, is a *château fort*

Donjon - castle keep

Bastide - several meanings : it can be a stronghold, a small fortified village or, in Provence, it can simply be another word for *mas*

Longère - a long, low farmhouse made of Breton granite

Maison bourgeoise and *maison de maître* - big, comfortable houses standing in quite large grounds and built for well-to-do members of the liberal professions, captains of industry, trade, etc

Maison paysanne - country cottage

Mas - a Provençal country house, usually long and low with old stone walls, pan-tiled roof and painted shutters

Maison vigneronne can be anything from a tiny vine-worker's cottage to a comfortable house owned by the estate manager or proprietor

Dépendance - outbuilding of *château*, farm etc

Brocante - secondhand (furniture)

Châtelain/e - lord/lady of the manor

Grand-père - grandfather

Jouer aux boules, pétanque - bowling game played with metal balls on a dirt surface

Mairie and *Hôtel de Ville* - town and city hall respectively

Potage/potager - vegetable soup/vegetable garden

Pommeau - alcoholic drink made from apples

Armagnac - fiery spirit of distilled grapes produced in Gascony, not to be confused with cognac!

Pressoir - Press for olives/grapes/apples

French words and expressions

Déguster means to taste, sample or savour and *une dégustation* is a tasting - of wine, oysters, any speciality. Note that it is NOT necessarily free

Toile de Jouy - classic French fabrics and wallpapers depicting romantic or pastoral scenes, usually in pink or blue on white background

Porcherie - pig sty

Chartreuse - charterhouse or Carthusian monastery

Pineau - a Charentes wine distilled with cognac, served chilled as an aperitif

Puys - Auvergnat dialect for 'peak'

Grand magasin - department store

Œil de boeuf - literally bull's eye window, i.e. small circular window

Lavoir - wash-house

Lit bâteau - literally 'boat bed', French sleigh bed. A bed, usually in walnut, with wooden sides

Halles - covered market

Truffe - truffle

Grange - barn

Feria (actually Spanish) - fiesta, festival

Cave - cellar

Domaine - estate, often referring to wine-grower's estate

Bergerie - shepherd's hut

Pigeonnier - pigeon-house or dovecot

Maison à colombage - timbered or half-timbered house typical of Normandy

Vélo (tout terrain) - (mountain) bike

Sentier de Grande Randonnée (GR) - long distance footpath

Randonneur - walker

Magnanerie - silk worm farm

Vigneron - wine-grower/producer

Cantou - fireplace

Armoire - wardrobe

Filature - mill, place where spinning is carried out

Pastis - Provence's aniseed spirit

Pisé - rammed earth or clay used to make floors or walls (also called *pisé de terre*)

Ferme auberge - restaurant on a farm, using home-reared/grown produce

Tips for travellers in France

- If you are not wedded to a mobile phone buy a phonecard (*télécarte*) on arrival; they are on sale at post offices and tobacconists' (*tabac*).

- Be aware of public holidays; many national museums and galleries close on Tuesdays, others close on Mondays (e.g. Monet's garden in Giverny) as do many country restaurants, and opening times may be different on the following days:

New Year's Day (1 January)   May Day (1 May)
Liberation 1945 (8 May)   Bastille Day (14 July)
Assumption (15 August)   All Saints (1 November)

2002 (& 2003) dates:

Easter Sunday   31 March (20 April)
Ascension Thursday   9 May (29 May)
Whit Sunday & Monday (Pentecost)   19 & 20 May (8 & 9 June)

- Beware also of the mass exodus over public holiday weekends, both the first day - outward journey - and the last - return journey.

Medical and emergency procedures

- If you are an EC citizen, have an E111 form with you for filling in after any medical treatment. You will subsequently receive a refund for only part of your payment, so it is advisable to take out private insurance.

- French emergency services are: the public service called SAMU or the Casualty Department (*Services des Urgences*) of a hospital; the private service is called SOS MÉDECINS.

Roads and driving

- Current speed limits are: motorways 130 kph (80 mph), RN national trunk roads 110 kph (68 mph), other open roads 90 kph (56 mph), in towns 50 kph (30 mph). The road police are very active and can demand on-the-spot payment of fines.

- One soon gets used to driving on the right but complacency leads to trouble; take special care coming out of car parks, private drives, narrow one-lane roads and coming onto roundabouts.

Directions in towns

The French drive towards a destination and use road numbers far less than we do. Thus, to find your way *à la française*, know the general direction you want to go, i.e. the towns your route goes through, and when you see *Autres Directions* or *Toutes Directions* in a town, forget road numbers, just follow towards the place name you're heading for or through.

Avoiding cultural confusion

En suite

'En suite' is not used in France to describe bathrooms off the bedroom and to do so can lead to confusion. To be clear, simply ask for a room *'avec salle de bains et wc'*.

Greetings and forms of address

We drop far more easily into first-name terms than the French. This reluctance on their part is not a sign of coldness, it's simply an Old National Habit, to be respected, we feel, like any other tribal ritual. So it's advisable to wait for the signal from them as to when you have achieved more intimate status.

The French do not say "*Bonjour Monsieur Dupont*" or "*Bonjour Madame Jones*" - this is considered rather familiar. They just say "*Bonjour Monsieur*" or "*Bonjour Madame*" - which makes it easy to be lazy about remembering people's names.

À table

Breakfast

There may be only a bowl or large cup and a teaspoon per person on the table. If so, you are expected to butter your bread on your hand or on the tablecloth (often the kitchen oilcloth) using the knife in the butter dish, then spread the jam with the jam spoon.

A well-bred English lady would never dream of 'dunking' her croissant, toast or teacake in her cup - it is perfectly acceptable behaviour in French society.

Lunch/dinner

Cutlery is laid concave face upwards in 'Anglo-Saxon' countries; in France it is proper to lay forks and spoons convex face upwards (crests are engraved accordingly). Do try and hold back your instinctive need to turn them over!

To the right of your plate, at the tip of the knife, you may find a knife-rest. This serves two purposes: to lay your knife on when you are not using it, rather than leaving it on your plate; to lay your knife *and* fork on (points downwards) if you are asked to *'garder vos couverts'* (keep your knife and fork) while the plates are changed - e.g. between starter and main dish.

Cheese comes *before* pudding in France - that's the way they do it! Cut a round cheese as you would cut a round cake - in triangular segments. When a ready-cut segment such as a piece of Brie is presented, the rule is to 'preserve the point', i.e. do not cut it straight across but take an angle which removes the existing point but makes another one.

Cycling in France

Two and a half times the size of the UK, France offers rich rewards to the cyclist: plenty of space, a superb network of minor roads with little traffic, and a huge diversity of landscapes, smells and terrains. You can choose the leafy forests and gently undulating plains of the North, or the jagged glacier-topped mountains of the Alps. Pedal through wafts of fermenting grapes in Champagne, resinous pines in the Midi, or spring flowers in the Pyrenees. You can amble slowly, stopping in remote villages for delicious meals or a *café au lait,* or pit yourself against the toughest terrains and cycle furiously.

You will also be joining in a national sport: bikes are an important part of French culture and thousands don their lycra and take to their bikes on summer weekends. (You can join the French cycle touring club on its organised trips if you wish - see under Useful Numbers section.) The country comes to a virtual standstill during the three-week *Tour de France* cycling race in July and the media is dominated by talk of who is the latest *maillot jaune* (literally 'yellow jersey' - the fellow in the lead). Cycling stars become national heroes and heroines with quasi-divine status.

Mountain bikes are becoming increasingly popular. They are known as VTTs (*vélos tout terrain*) and there is an extensive network of VTT trails, usually marked in purple. Cycles are available for hire in most towns and at most SNCF stations (useful as you can drop them off at another) and often offer special rates for a week's hire. The bikes are often not insured, however, so check if your travel insurance covers you for theft or damage.

When to go

Avoid July and August, if possible, as it's hot and the roads are at their busiest. The South is good from mid-March, except on high ground which may be snow-clad until the end of June. The North, which has a similar climate to Britain's, can be lovely from May onwards. Most other areas are suitable from April until October.

Cycling in France

Getting bikes to and through France

If you are using public transport, you can get your bicycle to France by air, by ferry or via the Channel Tunnel. Ferries carry bikes for nothing or for a maximum of £5 one way. British Airways and Air France take bikes  free. If you are travelling by Eurostar, you can store your bike in one of the guards' vans which have cycle-carrying hooks, with a potential capacity of up to eight bikes per train. To do this you need to reserve and pay extra.

If you are travelling on French railways, some stations accept bikes free of charge, while others require you to register your bike, buy it a separate ticket, and it will travel separately. For information as to which trains accept bikes, consult the website of the French railways (SNCF): www.sncf.com

A few mainline and most regional trains accept bikes free of charge and you can place them in the guard's van. These trains are indicated by a small bike symbol in the timetable. In the Paris area, you can take bikes on most trains except during rush hours. Certain central RER stations forbid the mounting of bikes onto trains. In the Rhône-Alps region, all local trains accept bikes free of charge. However, some trains limit the number of bikes to three.

Maps

The two big names are Michelin and the *Institut Géographique National* (IGN). For route-planning, IGN publishes a map of the whole of France showing mountain-biking and cycle tourism (No. 906). The best on-the-road reference maps are Michelin's yellow 1:200,000 Series. IGN publishes a Green Series at a scale of 1:100,000. For larger scale maps, go for IGN's excellent 1:25,000 Top 25 and Blue Series (which you will also use for walking). You can buy maps at most *Maisons de la Presse* newsagents in France, or at Stanfords in the UK.

Repairs and spare **parts**

Bike shops are at least as numerous as in Britain and you should be able to get hold of spare parts, provided you don't try between noon and 2pm, when shops close for the all important business of lunching. Prices are often lower than in Britain and the US. However, if you have a non-French bike with non-standard metric wheels, it's advisable to carry spare tyres.

Walking in France

With over 60,000 kilometres of clearly marked long distance footpaths, or *sentiers de Grandes Randonnées* (GRs for short), and a fantastic variety of landscapes and terrains, France is a superb country in which to walk. Hike in the snow-topped glaciers of the Northern Alps, walk through the lush and rugged volcanic 'moonscapes' of the Auvergne, or amble through the vineyards of Burgundy, Alsace or Provence.

Stroll for an afternoon, or make an odyssey over several months. Some long-distance walks have become classics, like the famous GR65, the pilgrim road to Santiago de Compostela, the *Tour du Mont Blanc*, or the 450 kilometre long GR3 *Sentier de la Loire*, which runs from the Ardèche to the Atlantic. Wild or tamed, hot or temperate, populated or totally empty, take your choice: France has it all.

Wherever you are renting a house, there will almost certainly be a GR near you. You can walk a stretch of it, then use other paths to turn it into a circular walk. As well as the network of GRs, marked with red and white parallel paint markings, there's a network of *Petites Randonnées* (PRs), usually signalled by single yellow or green paint stripes. In addition, there are *sentiers de Grandes Randonnées de Pays* (GRPs), marked by a red and yellow stripe, and any number of variants of the original GR route which eventually become paths in their own right. Paths are evolving all the time.

The paths are lovingly waymarked and maintained by the *Fédération Française de la Randonnée Pédestre* (FFRP), which was founded in 1947 under another name. The federation is also responsible for producing the topo-guides, books for walkers containing walking directions and maps (see under Books).

The great reward for walkers is that you'll penetrate the soul of rural France in a way you never could from a car. You'll see quaint ruined châteaux, meet country characters whom you'll never forget, and last but not least, you'll encounter a dazzling variety of flora and fauna if you look for it. France has a remarkably rich natural heritage, including 266 species of nesting birds, 131 species of mammal, and nearly 5,000 species of flowering plants. Look out for golden eagles, griffon vultures and marmots in the Alps and Pyrenees, red kites and lizard orchids in the Dordogne, and fulmars and puffins off the rocky Brittany coast. There's no room for complacency, however, as hundreds of species are threatened with extinction: 400 species of flora are classed as threatened and about 20 species of mammals and birds are vulnerable or in danger of extinction.

When to go

The best months for walking are May, June, September and October. In high mountain areas, summers are briefer and paths may be free of snow only between July and early September. In the northern half of France July and August are also good months, but it's too hot at this time of year in the South. Southern France is ideal for a winter break, when days are often crisp and clear.

Maps

As mentioned in the cycling section, the two big names for maps are IGN (*Institut Géographique National*) and Michelin. IGN maps are likely to be of most use for walkers. A useful map for planning walks is the IGN's *France: Grande Randonnée* sheet No. 903 which shows all the country's long distance footpaths. For walking, the best large-scale maps are the IGN's 1:25,000 *Serie Bleue* and Top 25 series. Also look out for IGN's 1:50,000 *Plein Air* series which includes GRs and PRs, plus hotels and campsites. Unfortunately they cover only limited areas.

Books

The FFRP produces more than 180 topo-guides, guidebooks for walkers which include walking instructions and IGN maps (usually 1:50,000). Most of these are now translated into English so it's worth buying one of these of the area where you are going before you leave. Consult its web site too.

The *Code du Randonneur*

Love and respect nature • Avoid unnecessary noise • Destroy nothing • Do not leave litter • Do not pick flowers or plants • Do not disturb wildlife Re-close all gates • Protect and preserve the habitat • No smoking or fires in the forests • Stay on the footpath • Respect and understand the country way of life and the country people • Think of others as you think of yourself

Clothing and equipment

This obviously depends on the terrain, the length of the walk and the time of year, but here's a suggested checklist:

Boots, sunhat, suncream and lip salve, mosquito repellent, sunglasses, sweater, cagoule, stick, water bottle, gaiters, change of clothing, phrase book, maps, compass, sense of humour, field guides to flora and fauna, waterproof daypack, camera and spare film, Swiss Army knife, whistle (for emergencies), spare socks, binoculars, waterproof jacket and trousers, emergency food, first-aid kit, torch.

Getting about in France

You'll probably expect to drive to your holiday home. However, being an environmentally-friendly company, we are keen to promote the use of public transport and have listed those properties which you can reach by train (in some cases owners are willing to collect you and your luggage - see Quick Reference Indices). We realise that if you have three children and suitcases of nappies, buckets and spades, public transport may simply not be an option. However, with the most extensive rail network in western Europe, France is a country in which it is surprisingly easy, restful and economical to travel by public transport. So do give it some thought.

Trains

France's nationally owned rail network, operated by the *Société Nationale des Chemins de Fer* (SNCF*)*, runs fast and efficient services to almost every part of the country, and in rural areas where branch lines have been closed, routes are covered by SNCF-operated buses. The SNCF offers a range of discount tickets, from couples to people over 60 to people between 12 and 25. Check if you are eligible and book well in advance.

The system's pride and joy, the TGV (*train à grande vitesse*), which travels at a maximum 300kph, covers three regional routes: the South-East (links Paris Gare de Lyons with Lyons, Dijon, Geneva, Alps, Avignon, Marseille, Nice and Perpignan); the Atlantic (links Paris Gare de Montparnasse with Brittany, Nantes, the Loire Valley, Bordeaux, the Pyrenees and Toulouse); the North (links Paris Gare du Nord with Lille and Calais.) You should book TGV trains in advance and remember to validate (*composter*) all tickets before boarding.

If you do need to take a car to the South of France, but don't relish the thought of a long tiring drive, you also have the option of Motorail. You check your car in at Calais and a train takes you and your car to your destination. Sleepers and couchettes are available, and it's cheaper if you travel mid-week. At the time of writing (autumn 2001), destinations linked by Motorail are: Brive, Toulouse, Narbonne, Avignon and Nice.

Buses

In additon to SNCF buses linking to trains, private buses cover local and cross-country routes and are usually geared around school and working hours. Enquire at the *gare routière* in most large towns.

Useful addresses & phone numbers

French tourist offices

UK:

178 Piccadilly, London W1V 0AL

Tel: +44 (0)9068 244123 Fax: +44 (0)20 74936594

E-mail: piccadilly@mdlf.demon.co.uk

New York:

444 Madison Ave, 16th floor, New York, NY10022-6903

Tel: +1 (0)212 838 7800 Fax: +1 (0)212 838 7855

E-mail: info@francetourism.com

Los Angeles:

9454 Wiltshire Blvd, Suite 715, Beverley Hills, CA 90212-2967

Tel: +1 (0)310 271 6665 Fax: +1 (0)310 276 2835

E-mail: fgtola@juno.com OR frenchtouristoffice@tinet.ie

Ireland:

10 Suffolk St, Dublin 2

Tel: +353 (0)1 679 0813 Fax: +353 (0)1 874 7324

E-mail: frenchtouristoffice@tinet.ie

French embassies

Britain:

58 Knightsbridge, London SW1X 7JT

Tel: +44 (0)20 7273 1000

Ireland:

36 Ailesbury Rd, Ballsbridge, Dublin 4

Tel: +353 (0)1 260 1666

US:

4101 Reservoir Rd NW, Washington DC 20007

Tel: +1 (0)202 944 6195

www.info-france-usa.org

Canada:

42 Sussex Drive, Ottawa, ON K1M 2C9

Tel: +1 (0)613 789 1795

www.amba-ottawa.fr

Useful addresses & phone numbers

Motoring

Eurotunnel: the sole Channel Tunnel operator offers a regular service from Folkstone to Calais. Pre-book during busy periods.
Tel: +44 (0)8705 353535
www.eurotunnel.com

Europ Assistance: offers help with car insurance. (Green cards are no longer compulsory, but are worth getting for fully comprehensive cover.)
Tel: +44 (0)1444 442211

Route and traffic information:
Autoroutel offers a multi-lingual service:
Tel: +33 (0)1 47 05 90 01
www.autoroutes.fr

For non-motorway routes:
www.mappy.fr

Ferry companies

Brittany Ferries (Portsmouth-Caen/St Malo; Poole-Cherbourg; Plymouth-Roscoff)
Tel: +44 (0)8705 360360
www.brittany-ferries.com

Condor Ferries (Weymouth/Poole-St Malo)
Tel: +44 (0)1305 761551
www.condorferries.co.uk

Hoverspeed (Dover-Calais; Folkstone-Boulogne; Newhaven-Dieppe)
Tel: +44 (0)870 524 0241
www.hoverspeed.co.uk

P&O Portsmouth (Portsmouth-Le Havre/Cherbourg)
Tel: +44 (0)870 242 4999

P&O Stena (Dover-Calais)
Tel: +44 (0)870 600 0600
www.posl.com

SeaFrance (Dover-Calais)
Tel: +44 (0)870 571 1711
www.seafrance.com

Useful addresses & phone numbers

Norfolkline (Dover-Dunkerque: no foot passengers, cars only)
Tel: +44 (0)1304 218410
www.norfolkline.com

Rail travel

SNCF's motorail can be booked through:
Rail Europe
179 Piccadilly, London W1
Tel: +44 (0)8705 848848
www.raileurope.co.uk

Rail Europe
226 Westchester Av, West Plains, NY 10064
Tel: +1 (0)800 438 7245
www.raileurope.com

Eurostar
Tel: +44 (0)8705 186 186
www.eurostar.com

Cycling

Cyclists' Touring Club in UK
Cotterell House, 68 Meadrow,
Godalming, Surrey GU7 3HS
Tel: +44 (0)1483 417217
Fax: +44 (0)1483 426994
E-mail: cycling@ctc.org.uk

Fédération Française de Cyclotourisme
12 rue Louis Bertrand, 94200 Ivry sur Seine
Tel: +33 (0)1 56 20 88 88
www.ffct.org

Walking

Fédération Française de la Randonnée Pédestre (FFRP)
14 rue Riquet, 75019 Paris
Tel:+33 (0)1 44 89 93 93
www.ffrp.asso.fr

L'Institut Géographique National (IGN)
136 bis, rue de Grenelle, Paris
Tel:+33 (0)1 43 98 80 00 Fax:+33 (0)1 43 98 85 11
www.ign.fr

Useful addresses & phone numbers

Maps

Michelin's yellow regional maps are readily available in French service stations or newsagents; also the excellent sheet map No. 989 which covers the whole country.

Stanfords
12-14 Long Acre, London WC2E 9LP
Tel: +44 (0)207 836 1321
29 Corn St, Bristol BS1 1HT
Tel: +44 (0)117 929 9966
www.stanfords.co.uk

Naturalists, ornithologists' contacts

Fédération des Parcs Naturels Régionaux de France
4 rue de Stockholm, 75008 Paris
Tel: +33 (0)1 44 90 86 20 Fax: +33 (0)1 45 22 70 78
E-mail: info@parcs-naturels-regionaux.tm.fr
www.parcs-naturels-regionaux.tm.fr
Website has up-to-date info including details of organised walks in parks.

La Ligue pour la Protection des Oiseaux,
Corderie Royale, BP 263, 17305 Rochefort
Tel: +33 (0)5 46 82 12 34 Fax: +33 (0)5 46 83 95 86
www.lpo-birdlife.asso.fr

Emergency numbers in France

Fire (Pompiers): 18
Ambulance (SAMU): 15
Police and Ambulance: 17

Weather forecast

www.meteo.fr

What is Alastair Sawday Publishing?

A dozen or more of us work in two converted barns on a farm near Bristol, close enough to the city for a bicycle ride and far enough for a silence broken only by horses and the occasional passage of a tractor. Some editors work in the countries they write about, e.g. France and Spain, others work from the UK but are based outside the office. We enjoy each other's company, celebrate every event possible, and work in an easy-going but committed environment.

These books owe their style and mood to Alastair's miscellaneous career and his interest in the community and the environment. He has taught overseas, worked with refugees, run development projects abroad and founded a travel company and several environmental organisations - many of which have flourished. There has been a slightly mad streak evident throughout, not least in his driving of a waste-paper-collection lorry for a year, the manning of stalls at impoverished jumble sales and the pursuit of causes long before they were considered sane.

Back to the travel company: trying to take his clients to eat and sleep in places that were not owned by corporations and assorted bandits he found dozens of very special places in France - farms, châteaux etc - a list that grew into the first book, *French Bed and Breakfast*. It was a celebration of 'real' places to stay and the remarkable people who run them.

The publishing company is based on the unexpected success of that first and rather whimsical French book. It started as a mild crusade, and there it stays - full of 'attitude', and the more appealing for it. For we still celebrate the unusual, the beautiful, the individual. We are passionate about rejecting the banal, the ugly, the pompous and the indifferent and we are passionate too about promoting the use of 'real' food. Alastair is a trustee of the Soil Association and keen to promote organic growing and consuming by owners and visitors.

It is a source of deep pleasure to us to have learned that there are many thousands of people who share our views. We are by no means alone in trumpeting the virtues of standing up to the destructive uniformity of so much of our culture.

We are building a company in which people and values matter. We love to hear of new friendships between those in the book and those using it, and to know that there are many people - among them farmers - who have been enabled to pursue their lives thanks to the extra income our books bring them.

Alastair Sawday's
Special Places to Stay series

www.specialplacestostay.com

The Little Earth Book - 2nd Edition

A fascinating read. The earth is now desperately vulnerable; so are we. Original, stimulating mini-essays about what is going wrong with our planet, and about the greatest challenge of our century: how to save the Earth for us all. It is pithy, yet intellectually credible, well-referenced, wry yet deadly serious.

Alastair Sawday, the publisher, is also an environmentalist. For over 25 years he has campaigned, not only against the worst excesses of modern tourism and its hotels, but against environmental 'looniness' of other kinds. He has fought for systems and policies that might enable our beautiful planet - simply - to survive. He founded and ran Avon Friends of the Earth, has run for Parliament, and has led numerous local campaigns. He is now a trustee of the Soil Association, experience upon which he draws in this remarkable book.

Researched and written by an eminent Bristol architect, James Bruges, *The Little Earth Book* is a clarion call to action, a mind-boggling collection of mini-essays on today's most important environmental concerns, from global warming and poisoned food to economic growth, Third World debt, genes and 'superbugs'. Undogmatic but sure-footed, the style is light, explaining complex issues with easy language, illustrations and cartoons. Ideas are developed chapter by chapter, yet each one stands alone. It is an easy browse.

The Little Earth Book provides hope, with new ideas and examples of people swimming against the current, of bold ideas that work in practice. It is a book as important as it is original. Learn about the issues and join the most important debate of this century.

Did you know.....

- If everyone adopted the Western lifestyle we would need five earths to support us

- In 50 years the US has - with intensive pesticide use - doubled the amount of crops lost to pests

- Environmental disasters have created more than 80 million refugees

www.thelittleearth.co.uk

www.specialplacestostay.com

Adrift on the unfathomable and often unnavigable sea of accommodation pages on the Internet, those who have discovered www.specialplacestostay.com have found it to be an island of reliability. Not only will you find a database full of honest, trustworthy, up-to-date information about over a thousand *Special Places to Stay* across Europe, but also:

- **Direct links to the web sites of hundreds of places from the series**
- **Colourful, clickable, interactive maps**
- **The facility to make most bookings by email -**
  even if you don't have email yourself
- **Online purchasing of our books, securely and cheaply**
- **Regular, exclusive special offers on books from the whole series**
- **The latest news about future editions, new titles and new places**
- **The chance to participate in the evolution of both the guides**
  and the site

The site is constantly evolving and is frequently updated. By the time you read this we will have introduced an online notice board for owners to use, where they can display special offers or forthcoming local events that might tempt you. We're expanding our European maps, adding more useful and interesting links, providing news, updates and special features that won't appear anywhere else but in our window on the world wide web.

Just as with our printed guides, your feedback counts, so when you've surfed all this and you still want more, let us know - this site has been planted with room to grow!

Russell Wilkinson, Web Editor
editor@specialplacestostay.com

Order Form UK

All these books are available in major bookshops or you may order them direct. Post and packaging are FREE.

	Price	No. copies
Special Places to Stay: **Portugal**		
Edition 1	£8.95	
Special Places to Stay: **Spain**		
Edition 4	£11.95	
Special Places to Stay: **Ireland**		
Edition 3	£10.95	
Special Places to Stay: **Paris Hotels**		
Edition 3	£8.95	
Special Places to Stay: **Garden Bed & Breakfast**		
Edition 1	£10.95	
Special Places to Stay: **French Bed & Breakfast**		
Edition 7	£14.99	
Special Places to Stay: **British Hotels, Inns and Other Places**		
Edition 3	£11.99	
Special Places to Stay: **British Bed & Breakfast**		
Edition 6	£13.95	
Special Places to Stay: **French Hotels, Inns and Other Places**		
Edition 2	£11.99	
Special Places to Stay: **Italy**		
Edition 2	£11.95	
Special Places to Stay: **French Holiday Homes**		
Edition 1	£11.99	
The Little Earth Book	£5.99	

Please make cheques payable to: **Alastair Sawday Publishing**   **Total** [   ]

Please send cheques to: Alastair Sawday Publishing, The Home Farm Stables, Barrow Gurney, Bristol BS48 3RW. **For credit card orders call 01275 464891 or order directly from our website www.specialplacestostay.com**

Name:

Address:

Postcode:

Tel: Fax: FSC1

If you do not wish to receive mail from other companies, please tick the box ❏

Order Form USA

All these books are available at your local bookstore, or you may order
direct. Allow two to three weeks for delivery.

	Price	No. copies
Special Places to Stay: Portugal		
Edition 1	$14.95	
Special Places to Stay: Ireland		
Edition 3	$17.95	
Special Places to Stay: Spain		
Edition 4	$19.95	
Special Places to Stay: Paris Hotels		
Edition 3	$14.95	
Special Places to Stay: French Bed & Breakfast		
Edition 7	$19.95	
Special Places to Stay: British Bed & Breakfast		
Edition 6	$19.95	
Special Places to Stay: Garden Bed & Breakfast		
Edition 1	$17.95	
Special Places to Stay: Italy		
Edition 2	$17.95	
Special Places to Stay: British Hotels, Inns and Other Places		
Edition 3	$17.95	
Special Places to Stay: French Hotels, Inns and Other Places		
Edition 2	$19.95	

Shipping in the continental USA: $3.95 for one book,
$4.95 for two books, $5.95 for three or more books.
Outside continental USA, call (800) 243-0495 for prices.
For delivery to AK, CA, CO, CT, FL, GA, IL, IN, KS, MI, MN, MO, NE,
NM, NC, OK, SC, TN, TX, VA, and WA, please add appropriate sales tax.

Please make checks payable to: The Globe Pequot Press   **Total**

To order by phone with MasterCard or Visa: (800) 243-0495. 9a.m. to 5p.m.
EST; by fax: (800) 820-2329, 24 hours; through our web site:
www.globe-pequot.com; or by mail: The Globe Pequot Press, P.O. Box 480,
Guilford, CT 06437.

Name: _____ Date: _____

Address: _____

Town: _____

FSC1 State: _____ Zip code: _____

Tel: _____ Fax: _____

Report Form

Comments on existing entries and new discoveries.

If you have any comments on entries in this guide, please let us have them.
If you have a favourite house, hotel, inn or other new discovery, not just in
France, please let us know about it.

Book title: Entry no: Edition:

New recommendation   Country:

Name of property:

Address:

                                   Postcode:

Tel:

Date of stay:

Comments:

From:

Address:

                                   Postcode:

Tel:

Please send the completed form to: **Alastair Sawday Publishing,
The Home Farm Stables, Barrow Gurney, Bristol BS48 3RW** or go to
www.specialplacestostay.com and click on contact.

Thank you.

Shorten

lengthen

CORK

POOLE PORTSMOUTH

PLYMOUTH

CHERBOURG

CAEN

ROSCOFF ST.MALO

SANTANDER

Information & booking
0870 908 1284